WHISTLEBLOWING

WHISTLEBLOWING

Managing Dissent in the Workplace

by
Frederick Elliston
John Keenan
Paula Lockhart
and Jane van Schaick

PRAEGER

PRAEGER SPECIAL STUDIES • PRAEGER SCIENTIFIC

New York • Philadelphia • Eastbourne, UK
Toronto • Hong Kong • Tokyo • Sydney

658.314
W 576

Library of Congress Cataloging in Publication Data

Main entry under title:

Whistleblowing: managing dissent in the workplace.

Includes bibliographies and index.
1. Whistle blowing—United States. I. Elliston,
Frederick.
HD60.5.U5W473   1984   658.3′14   84-13294
ISBN 0-03-070774-9 (alk. paper)
ISBN 0-03-070776-5 (pbk. : alk. paper)

Published in 1985 by Praeger Publishers
CBS Educational and Professional Publishing, a Division of CBS Inc.
521 Fifth Avenue, New York, NY 10175 USA

56789 052 987654321

Printed in the United States of America on acid-free paper

INTERNATIONAL OFFICES

Orders from outside the United States should be sent to the appropriate address listed below. Orders from areas not listed below should be placed through CBS International Publishing, 383 Madison Ave., New York, NY 10175 USA

Australia, New Zealand
Holt Saunders, Pty, Ltd., 9 Waltham St., Artarmon, N.S.W. 2064, Sydney, Australia

Canada
Holt, Rinehart & Winston of Canada, 55 Horner Ave., Toronto, Ontario, Canada M8Z 4X6

Europe, the Middle East, & Africa
Holt Saunders, Ltd., 1 St. Anne's Road, Eastbourne, East Sussex, England BN21 3UN

Japan
Holt Saunders, Ltd., Ichibancho Central Building, 22-1 Ichibancho, 3rd Floor, Chiyodaku, Tokyo, Japan

Hong Kong, Southeast Asia
Holt Saunders Asia, Ltd., 10 Fl, Intercontinental Plaza, 94 Granville Road, Tsim Sha Tsui East, Kowloon, Hong Kong

Manuscript submissions should be sent to the Editorial Director, Praeger Publishers, 521 Fifth Avenue, New York, NY 10175 USA

ACKNOWLEDGMENTS

Our work was supported by a grant (NSF #OSS-8006553) from a program on Ethical Values in Science and Technology, jointly sponsored by the National Endowment for the Humanities and the National Science Foundation. We gratefully acknowledge this support.

As well, we would like to thank the members of the Michael Hindelang Research Center at the State University of New York at Albany for their patience and advice and the members of the Center for the Study of Ethics in the Professions at the Illinois Institute of Technology for their suggestions and assistance.

CONTENTS

LIST OF ABBREVIATIONS

AAUP	American Association of University Professors
ACPAS	Accounts Payable System
AEC	Atomic Energy Commission
BART	Bay Area Rapid Transit
EPA	Environmental Protection Agency
FFA	Federal Financing Administration
FLRA	Federal Labor Relations Authority
FPA	Farm and Produce Administration
IEEE	The Institute of Electrical and Electronic Engineers
MCC	Membership Conduct Committee
MHPC	Municipal Health Planning Council
MSPB	Merit Systems Protection Board
NASA	National Aeronautics and Space Administration
OIG	Office of Inspector General
OPM	Office of Personnel Management
OSC	Office of Special Counsel
OSHA	Occupational Safety and Health Act
PAMOS	Patient Monitoring System
QA	Quality Assurance
VCC	Virginia Chemical Company

INTRODUCTION

Whistleblowing has received considerable attention in the media via regular newspaper stories, magazine articles, and television documentaries. It has eclipsed political protest as a newsworthy item, and for good reason. The whistleblowers of the 1970s and 1980s bear the mantle worn by the civil disobedients of the 1960s, shifting the object of dissent from government atrocities in Vietnam to corporate wrongdoing in the workplace.

Much of the literature to date has been anecdotal. People tell their tales of growing suspicions, secret investigations, attempted disclosures, and subsequent harassment. It is only during the last few years that whistleblowing has come to attract the attention of academics.[1]

Legal scholars have focused on the employment-at-will doctrine and the rights of employees under collective bargaining agreements, the common-law tradition, recent state and federal statutes, and the First Amendment. Students and critics of public administration and public affairs have examined the mechanisms within state and federal agencies to control waste and to protect those who disclose it. And a growing number of social scientists have looked at the causes of discontent in terms of organizational and psychological factors.

As we entered this arena, we felt a tension in the very focus on the subject matter. What were we examining — the individual whistleblower, the act of blowing the whistle or the organization on which the whistle was blown? In the end we decided it was none of these. Rather, we decided to look at strategies. The primary question addressed in this volume is not who blows the whistle; it is not what they blow the whistle on; and it is not why they do so. As a distinct approach, we elected to examine the means, both inside and outside the organization, to resolve differences in professional judgment. Ours, therefore, is a strategic analysis.

We found the very notion of whistleblowing problematic and ambiguous. A number of conceptual questions needed to be answered and no clear answer was provided in the popular or scholarly literature. Must one go outside the organization to be counted as a whistleblower, or does it suffice that one goes outside the normal channels of communication within the organization? Attempts to answer this question lead inevitably to another. How does one draw the boundaries of the organization: Do shareholders, corporate ombudsmen, inspectors general, or consultants count as "members"? Does it matter what one's intentions are — ambition, revenge, justice — to the categorization of an individual as a whistleblower? Does it make a difference what the evidence is, whether the allegations are correct or warranted, and whether the individual succeeds or fails either in attracting attention or in correcting the wrong? And in the final analysis, what difference does it make how one answers these questions?

The fact is that people disagree, and somehow they must work out their differences. A variety of techniques are available for reaching a working arrangement and we decided to focus on these.

Altogether we identified seven avenues of dissent: consultants, community action groups, the media, professional associations, the inspectors general, the courts and Congress. Some work better than others, for the individual, the organization, or both. Their effectiveness depends on the particular issue, the structure of the organization, the personal predilections of the protagonists, their role in the organization, and the alternatives available. In the final chapter we have reflected on some lessons for prospective whistleblowers — precautions they would do well to take, problems they would do well to anticipate, and costs they would do well to weigh. And we offer some advice to organizations who seek to avoid the embarrassment of employees' raising allegations of wrongdoing: we identify mechanisms for avoiding confrontations, anticipating troublesome incidents, and identifying places within the organization where dissent is most likely to occur.

The cases presented are factual; they are based on interviews with members of various organizations. To protect the identity of those who asked to remain anonymous, we have fictionalized all of the names. But we have taken pains to preserve the character of the incident, the issues, the conflicts, the personalities of the protagonists, and the nature of the strategy and outcome.

Each working environment develops its own standard operating procedures, its own set of overlapping goals, and its own means of accommodating conflicts among them and among the groups that pursue them. None of these is cast in stone; each has its own history and evolves to meet changing circumstances, both internal and external. So one of our objectives has been to illuminate these various corporate cultures and institutional contexts.

We have brought a critical perspective to bear on both the tactics used to deal with dissent and the organizational setting within which it arises. We have sought to identify the underlying ethical principles, their implications, and their interconnections. The result is not a purely descriptive work but one that is self-confessedly prescriptive. We have not avoided taking a controversial stance or passing judgments: we have taken the moral point of view. To do otherwise would suggest that all viewpoints are of equal merit. Although each individual has the right to his or her opinion, it does not follow that each opinion is right. Certainly they cannot all be right when they do not agree. Nor can we judge the correct moral stance on the basis of which one prevails — the doctrine that might is right. Rather, we must try to appreciate the consequences for the organization, its members, and the society at large. It is on the basis of this sense of the institutional and social order that we have sought to address the moral issues and to articulate and defend our stance on them.

The result is not intended as a self-help book or guide to prospective whistleblowers, though we hope that both employees and employers will find it instructive. It is intended primarily to illuminate the problem of employee rights, and the means for resolving conflicts among them.

NOTE

1. For a summary of the scholarly literature, see James Bowman, Frederick Elliston, and Paula Lockhart, *Professional Dissent: An Annotated Bibliography and Resource Guide* (New York: Garland, 1983).

PART ONE
THE HISTORICAL BACKDROP

ONE
THE LAW
AND THE STATE

Emerging with the increased concern for employee rights are a growing number of limitations on employers' relatively unchecked discharge power. These recent developments are both statutory and judicial in nature: they are the result of laws enacted by state and federal governments and the growing body of case law emanating from the common law and recent court decisions. Without these protections from abusive employer power, employees are subject to demotion, transfer, or dismissal.

However, a few innovative organizations have initiated mechanisms to enable professionals to voice their concerns. They encourage professionals to bring to management's attention violations of safety standards or government regulations.

THE COMMON-LAW TRADITION

The employment relationship has, until recently, been governed by the employment-at-will doctrine. This doctrine is based on the premise that the employment contract is terminable at will by either party at any time and for any reason. Therefore, common law permits employers to dismiss their employees at will even for cause morally wrong without being guilty of any wrongdoing.[1]

Within the last few years, however, a handful of state courts have created an exception to the employment-at-will doctrine based upon the social good.[2] The origin of this exception is found in the court decision of *Petermann v. International Brotherhood of Teamsters*.[3] The court explicitly ruled that the right of an employer to discharge an at-will employee must be limited "by considerations

7

of public policy."[4] *Petermann* involved an employee who refused to commit perjury before a state legislative committee and alleged that the only reason for his termination was retaliation for his refusal to give false testimony. The California Court of Appeals held that the termination gave rise to a cause of action for wrongful discharge.[5]

Subsequent cases that have developed the public policy exception tend to fall into one of three categories, depending on the source of the determinant of public policy.[6] First, a statute may grant a right to the discharged employee and impose a corresponding duty on the employer, and yet remain silent as to the means of enforcing the right. The courts must determine if the statute intends that a private remedy be implied when an employer has attempted to contravene public policy.[7] Second, a statute may express a public policy that the employer has breached but provide neither a right nor a remedy for the terminated at-will employee. It is then up to the courts to imply both.[8] Third, in the absence of legislative expression of a public policy covering the circumstances of the discharged employee, the employee must seek judicial implication of a right and a remedy. In this category the judiciary must also define public policy.[9]

In sum, the employee is required to show that through the exercise of retaliatory discharge power the employer has breached societal interests and violated public policy. However, private at-will employees who have been dismissed for blowing the whistle on their organizations or for refusing to engage in illegal or unethical conduct have not generally fared well in the courts.[10]

Only thirteen jurisdictions recognize a cause of action in tort for wrongful discharge.[11] According to Alfred Feliu,[12] these courts, after considering the merits of the case, have weighed four factors in their decision: 1) the substantiality of the relevant public policy;[13] 2) where and in what context it was announced;[14] 3) how it fares when weighed against the employer's and society's broader interests;[15] and 4) whether the violation of the public policy in the case was so offensive as to warrant an exception to the employment-at-will doctrine.[16]

STATE AND FEDERAL STATUTES

Several recently enacted federal statutes contain antireprisal provisions that afford protection to employees. Congress enacted these special protection provisions because of the growing concern for the unchecked discriminatory power of the employer. Proponents of this legislation argue that unless whistleblowers are protected, serious health and safety violations will go unreported. These statutes fall into two categories: the occupational health and safety legislation and the environmental laws. The former category includes the Occupational Safety and Health Act (OSHA)[17], the Federal Mine Safety and Health Act[18], the Longshoremen's and Harbor Workers Act[19], and the Atomic Energy Act.[20] Examples in the latter category include the Federal Water Pollution Control Act[21], the Water Pollution Control Act,[22] the Toxic Substances Act[23], the Clean Air Act,[24] and the Surface Mining Reclamation Act[25]. Employees are protected when they bring violations to the attention of the appropriate authorities. Any employee who believes he or she has been discriminated against by an employer may file a complaint with the Department of Labor. But the employee frequently has only 30 days in which to file[26].

Several states have recently passed "whistleblower bills," which forbid employers to take reprisals against employees who report violations of the law to authorities.[27]

Michigan's whistleblower bill, enacted in early 1981, is the first in the nation to protect both private and public employees. It forbids employers from taking reprisals against any employee who has given, or is about to give, information to authorities concerning possible violations of the law. Any employee who believes that an employer has violated the act may commence an action in circuit court. Once in court the individual has to prove that the employer did indeed fire or otherwise discriminate against the individual because he or she blew the whistle. If the court finds in the employee's favor, it could order the employee reinstated along with the payment of back wages, full reinstatement of fringe benefits and seniority rights, reimbursement for actual damages, or any combination of these. Should the judge find in favor of the employer, the judge could order the employee to pay court costs including the employer's attorney fees. A person who violates this act is subject to a civil fine of not more than $500.

The Maryland law enacted prior to the Michigan bill, in July 1980, empowers the state secretary of personnel to bring sanctions against any manager who attempts reprisals against a public employee for disclosing information either publicly or privately. The law, however, does not require any investigation into the underlying charges of wrongdoing — an apparent weakness.

A measure passed by California in 1979 offers protection only to those whistleblowers who testify before special legislative committees — a limited but still helpful protection. It is too early to tell whether these laws will be truly effective in protecting employees.

REFORM LEGISLATION

In 1978 the Civil Service Commission was abolished by the Civil Service Reform Act.[28] The change was initiated as the result of a growing awareness of the difficulties encountered by the commission as a result of its conflicting responsibilities. It was charged with managing all personnel matters and protecting federal employees against their managers' actions. This conflict resulted in the creation of three new agencies: the Federal Labor Relations Authority (FLRA), the Merit Systems Protection Board (MSPB), and the Office of Personnel Management (OPM).

The FLRA acts as a referee in labor-management disputes. To stay abreast of unfair labor practices cases, the FLRA encourages informal, lower-level settlements.

The OPM, on the other hand, handles appeals and takes care of hiring, promotions, pay, and other personnel functions. Sponsors of the reform bill hoped to separate personnel management from the handling of employee complaints and judgment of violations,

The third element of President Jimmy Carter's civil service reform plan, the MSPB, handles employees' complaints and tries to protect government whistleblowers who expose wrongdoing. Within the framework of the new board, the Office of Special Counsel (OSC) was established in January 1979.[29]

The MSPB and the OSC were given separate authorities and responsibilities. The OSC is a semi-autonomous office. However, since the establishment of these offices, a number of questions regarding the relationship between the Board and the OSC have been raised. The OSC does have regulatory and management control over its operations, but it does not have independent budget authority.

The act requires that the OSC review alleged violations of laws, rules, or regulations; mismanagement; gross waste of funds; abuse of authority; or a substantial and specific danger to public health and safety. If the OSC determines that there is a likelihood of a violation, it may order that an investigation be made and a written report be forwarded to the agency head, to Congress, and to the OSC within 60 days. If an investigation is not warranted, the head of the agency is still required to notify the OSC in writing within 60 days of any action taken, or to be taken, and when such action will be completed. The employee making the allegation must also be notified.

In addition to initiating agency investigations, the OSC also has the responsibility of protecting those employees who disclose information concerning agency wrongdoing. If there are reasonable grounds to believe that retaliation has occurred, the OSC can request the MSPB to stay the practice and can bring disciplinary actions against those who take reprisals against government employees.

Overall, the act offers a number of advantages over the previous system. First, all employees are guaranteed by statute certain procedural rights in case of an adverse action. Second, appellants can recover attorney fees under certain circumstances.[30] Third, whistleblowers can solicit the assistance of the OSC before or after any retaliatory action.[31] Fourth, protected disclosures now encompass charges involving no crime. An employee may complain of mismanagement, gross waste of funds, abuse of authority, or substantial and specific danger to public health and safey.

In that same year President Carter signed a bill that reorganized the executive branch of the government by establishing Offices of Inspector General within 12 federal departments and agencies. Public Law 95-452 or the Inspector General Act of 1978, as it is commonly called, consolidated existing auditing and investigative resources to combat, more effectively, fraud, abuse, waste, and mismanagement in the programs and operations of those departments and agencies.

The concept of the inspector general is based on the premise that for the audit and investigative capacity to be effective authority must be vested in one individual who reports directly to the head of the agency and is under that person's supervision alone. The act not only mandates this autonomy but further states that the head of the agency may not prohibit, prevent, or limit the inspector general from undertaking and completing any audits and investigations that the inspector general deems necessary.

This legislation created positions of inspector general in the Departments of Agriculture, Commerce, Housing and Urban Development, the Interior, Labor, and Transportation and within the Community Services Administration, the National Aeronautics and Space Administration, the General Services Administration, the Environmental Protection Agency, the Veterans Administration, and the Small Business Administration. Their duties and responsibilities include: (1) providing policy direction for the auditing and investigative activities of the agency; (2) reviewing existing and proposed legislation and regulations relating to programs and operations of the agency and to Congress concerning the enforceability of such legislation; (3) supervising other activities for the purpose of promoting economy, efficiency, and effectiveness in the administration of such programs or for the purpose of preventing or detecting fraud and abuse in such programs; (4) coordinating relationships between the agency and other federal agencies, state and local governmental agencies, and non-governmental entities; and (5) keeping the head of the agency and Congress fully and currently informed concerning fraud and other serious problems in the operation of programs.[32]

In addition to investigating mismanagement, waste, or fraud, the inspector general may receive and investigate complaints or information from an employee of the agency concerning abuse of authority or a substantial and specific danger to the public health and safety. Moreover, the Civil Service Reform Act of 1978 requires that if a complaint is brought to the attention of the OSC, he or she should refer the complaint to the agency head for investigation. Consequently, the inspector general may receive not only complaints from employees but also those that come indirectly from the OSC via the agency head. Both the Inspector General Act and the Civil Service Reform Act protect the complaining employee by stipulating that the inspector general and the OSC not disclose the complainant's identity unless they determine that such disclosure is unavoidable during the course of the investigation. Furthermore, no employee is to suffer retaliation as a result of making a complaint or disclosing information to these government officials.

NOTES

1. Two of the earliest statements of the employment-at-will doctrine were those of the Tennessee Supreme Court in *Payne v. Western & Atlantic R.R. Co.*, 81 Tenn. 507 (1884), overruled on other grounds; and *Hutton v. Watters*, 132 Tenn. 527, 179 S.W. 134 (1915).
2. Note, "Implied Contractual Rights to Job Security," *Stanford Law Review* 26 (1974), 335.
3. For a review of the constitutional protection of the employment interest, see Cornelius J. Peck, "Unjust Discharges from Employment: A Necessary Change in the Law," *Ohio State Law Journal* 40 (1979), 1–49.
4. 344 P. 2d 25 (1959).
5. Id. at 28.
6. John Conway, "Protecting the Private Sector At-Will Employee Who Blows the Whistle: A Cause of Action Based Upon Determinants of Public Policy," *Wisconsin Law Review* 77 (1977): 777–812, sup. n. 18.
7. Id. at 789. See *Framptom v. Central Indiana Gas Co.*, 297 N.E. 2d 425 (1973) and

Sventko v. Kroger Co., 245 N.W. 2d 151 (1976), which both exemplify this approach.

8. See *Petermann*, sup. n. 28, which serves well as an example of the implication of both a right and a remedy.

9. Courts have responded in either of two ways: by modifying the doctrine of employment at will *(Monge v. Beebe Rubber Co.*, 316 A. 2d 549 (1974) or by creating a narrowly defined exception based upon a specific public policy *(Nees v. Hocks*, 536 P. 2d 512 [1975].

10. See *Geary v. United States Steel Co.*, 319 A. 2d 174 (1974) and *Percival v. General Motors Corporation*, 400 F. Supp. 1322 (E.D. Mo. 1975), aff'd, 539 F. 2d 1126 (18th Cir. 1976).

11. See Alfred Feliu, "Discharge of Professional Employees: Protecting against Dismissal for Acts within a Professional Code of Ethics," *Columbia Human Rights Law Review* 11 (1980):1 149–87. The jurisdictions are Arizona, California, Illinois, Indiana, Kentucky, Massachusetts, Michigan, New Hampshire, New Jersey, Oregon, Pennsylvania, Washington, and West Virginia.

12. Id. at 155.

13. *Campbell v. Ford Industries*, 274 Or. 243, 546 P. 2d 141 (1976) and *Beckett v. Welton & Associates*, 39 Cal. App. 3d 815, 114 Cal. Rptr. 531 (1974).

14. Id.

15. *Monge*, sup. n. 33.

16. *Pierce v. Ortho Pharmaceutical Corp.*, 166 N.J. Super. 335, 338, 399 A. 2d 1023, 1024 (1979), cert. granted 81 N.J. 266, 405 A. 2d 810 (1979).

17. 29 U.S.C. Sections 651–678 (1976). For an analysis of the act see Lewis Solomon and Terry Garcia, "Protecting The Corporate Whistleblower under Federal Anti-Reprisal Statutes." *Journal of Corporation Law* 5 (1980):1 275–297.

18. 30 U.S.C. Sections 801–960 (1976); amended by the Federal Mine Safety and Health Act of 1977, Section 102(a), 30 U.S.C. 801 (Supp. I 1977).

19. 33 U.S.C. Section 901 (1976).

20. 42 U.S.C. Sections 201–2296 (1976).

21. 33 U.S.C. Section 1251 (1976) (amended 1977).

22. 42 U.S.C. Section 330F (1976).

23. Occupational Safety and Health Act, Section 10(a), 29 U.S.C. Section 659(a) (1976).

24. 42 U.S.C. Section 7401 (1976).

25. 30 U.S.C. Section 1201 (Supp. I 1977).

26. Of the statutes mentioned, only the Federal Mine Safety and Health Act allows the individual sixty days within which to file a complaint.

27. E.G., *Conn. Gen. Stat. Ann.* 48–61DD(a) (1979), applies to public employees only; *Md. Ann. Code Art.* 64 Section 12 (1980), applies to public employees only; *Louisiana St. Labor Laws* 28 Section 1074.1(2) (1981), applies to both public and private employees; *Mich. Code Laws Ann.* 15.361 (1980), applies to both public and private employees; and *Cal. Labor Code* Section 432.2 and *Cal. Penal Code* Section 637.3 (1979), applies only to employees who testify before a joint legislative committee.

28. Public Law 95–454 (1978).

29. General Accounting Office, *The Office of OSC Can Improve Its Management of Whistleblower Cases* (Washington, D.C.: U.S. Government Printing Office, 1980), app. I, p. 1.

30. 5 U.S.C.A. Section 7701(g) (West Supp. 1979).

31. 5 U.S.C.A. Section 1206 (a) (1) (West Supp. 1979).

32. Public Law 95–452.

TWO
THREE MODELS

THE PROBLEM OF WHISTLEBLOWING

Within most organizations disgruntled employees have little recourse. They can voice their concerns to their superiors and risk retaliation. They can blow the whistle and jeopardize their jobs. They can suffer in silence and do nothing.

While most organizations have some type of "open door" appeal to management, the traditional chain of appeal is concerned mostly with internal and not external matters, employee grievances rather than public safety.

Yet a few innovative organizations have initiated mechanisms to enable professionals to voice their concerns. They encourage employees to bring to management's attention violations of safety standards or government regulations. Three such organizations that foster discussion and dissent through the use of such internal mechanisms are General Electric's Aircraft Engine Group, the Nuclear Regulatory Commission, and Avco-Everett Research Laboratory. All assert that the successful resolution of conflicting professional opinions must have the full support of management.

GENERAL ELECTRIC'S AIRCRAFT ENGINE GROUP

The Aircraft Engine Group (AEG) is one of ten operating groups in the General Electric (GE) Company. Headquartered at Lynn, Massachusetts, it has approximately 3,500 engineers, administrators, managers and other professionals and 4,000 technicians, semi-skilled and unskilled employees. Including Lynn, there are five additional plants for a total of 25,750 AEG employees.

Gerhard Neuman, the group executive and vice president for the AEG, joined GE in 1948. An outgoing and charismatic individual, Neuman prided himself on having rapport with his employees. However, as the AEG grew from a business with only a few hundred employees to an organization with thousands of employees, his personal contact with employees was severely constrained. Informal as Neuman's frequent "shop walks and talks" were, without them professional employees who were not represented by a union were left with no channels for resolving their disagreements.

Another factor that necessitated a formal avenue of dissent was the nature of their business venture. The AEG relied on the defense sector for most of their work. Managers were so concerned with meeting critical deadlines that even when a factual dispute was brought to their attention, they had little time to investigate it. As a consequence many important issues were never addressed — much less resolved.

In 1973 Neuman hired an ombudsman, a role originated by the Swedish government in 1809 for inquiry into complaints against administrative officials. According to Dr. Fredericka Dunn, an international personnel specialist and the first ombudsman for the AEG, Neuman expected the program to serve several functions: (1) to review administrative practices and develop programs to correct deficiencies; (2) to help evaluate progress of personnel programs; (3) to suggest improved communication techniques; (4) to report valid complaints to appropriate agencies; and (5) to serve as an impartial outlet for an employee's dissatisfaction with decisions adverse to him or her.

During the first year alone, 300 cases were brought to the ombudsman's attention and investigated. Well over half of them dealt with promotional opportunities and job search. Dunn also found that employees were receiving termination notices without adequate explanations. Other complaints typically involved performance appraisals, discrimination, patent disputes, and working conditions.

The first order of business, based on the sheer number of complaints about promotional opportunities, was to conduct an in-depth analysis into the way professional jobs were filled. An employee panel studied the whole area for approximately one year and proposed a Professional Staffing System, still in operation, which relies on posting all open positions exempt from union jurisdiction.

Well over two-thirds of all complaints are successfully resolved. Success is evidenced by the fact that a majority of the cases have been referred by persons who have had contact with the ombudsman themselves. Take, for example, the professional dispute that involved a disagreement between two engineers over the ownership of a patent. Dunn initiated an investigation after she received the complaint from an engineer who felt wronged when the company gave patent credit to another individual. He had been referred by an engineer who had been in a similar position. She was able to have the decision reversed and the engineer received proper credit for the patent.

Dunn attributes the success of the program to several factors. First, the ombudsman acts as a catalyst so that facts are clarified and adequately addressed. Second, the possibility of criticism by the ombudsman encourages administrators to make certain that they can justify their actions. Employees now have a formal channel of dissent that is assured by the full support of management. Third, at the AEG the ombudsman's position is given both high visibility and authority. The ombudsman is completely independent and functions as the eyes and ears of the president. He or she is seen by the members of the organization as representing the final decision-maker. To date, no one has suffered retaliation for using this office. Dunn believes it succeeds because managers view the ombudsman as an aid to reducing their workload rather than as an adversary.

The ombudsman's office has not been used to resolve purely technical disagreements thus far, although there is nothing in the program that would prevent employees from seeking the ombudsman's help in technical disputes. Ramona Martinez, the current ombudsman, like her predecessor, is involved in similar personnel-related problems.

Rick Haskel identified one possible reason. The AEG has a Design Review Board, which periodically reviews new designs and concepts and makes a determination on the product's integrity. This is one avenue through which contrary technical opinions are aired. During the rigorous review, disputes surface and are worked out rather informally.

THE NUCLEAR REGULATORY COMMISSION

On November 3, 1976, Ben C. Rusche, director of the Office of Nuclear Reactor Regulation (NRR), issued Office Letter #11 which sought to document and codify policy and practices for resolving technical issues.

If a staff member did not agree with the staff position, he or she was instructed first to discuss the disagreement with his or her section leader or branch chief in branches without section leaders. If the disagreement was not satisfactorily resolved, the dissenting employee could continue to appeal to higher levels — through the branch chief and the appropriate assistant director(s). Once it reached this level, the employee was required to prepare a memorandum concerning the technical issue and forward it to both the appropriate division director and to the director of NRR. The division director, in consultation with the director would make a final decision and notify the employee in writing. After completion of these steps, all relevant documents and written statements were to be sent to the Advisory Committee on Reactor Safeguards (ACRS) and placed in the Public Document Room. No one was to suffer retribution or recrimination as a result of using these procedures.

However, in 1978 several Nuclear Regulatory Commission employees testified before the Senate Committee on Government Affairs on the ineffectiveness of these procedures. Employees had been transferred and others had resigned after going public with technical concerns, charges of suppression of information and important safety issues.

NUREG-0567, released by the NRC in 1979, contained a plan entitled Proposed Policy and Procedures for Differing Professional Opinions. This plan was criticized by the Government Accountability Project (GAP) — a public interest group that supports federal whistleblowers, the American Civil Liberties Union (ACLU), and the American Association for the Advancement of Science. First, the NRC plan required that dissenting employees convey their disagreements in written signed statements to their immediate supervisor, ignoring the fact that the supervisor might be the source of the problem. This procedure could not ensure anonymity. Second, there was no requirement for timely resolution of significant issues concerning nuclear safety. The supervisor was required to provide monthly status reports to the employee but there was no provision for review by the public of the employee's objections or management's response. Third, in a letter to the NRC, GAP Director Louis Clark maintained, "To relegate the proposed system to a NUREG or a letter to the staff would implicitly downplay the NRC commitment to a full airing of scientific disputes." He argued that the regulations should be included in the NRC manual. Fourth, the GAP and the ACLU criticized the standard proposed by NRC for determining whether a dissident had been subjected to the agency's mission. These may involve technical, managerial, legal or policy issues. The NRC defines a "differing professional opinion" as a "conscientious expression of a professional judgment which, on any matter relating to NRC's mission or organizational activities, differs from the prevailing staff view within an organization, disagrees with a management decision or policy position, or takes issue with a proposed or an established agency practice."

The primary channel for expressing a differing professional opinion is through a signed statement by the dissenting employee submitted to his or her immediate supervisor. Upon receiving the written statement, the immediate supervisor must acknowledge receipt by memorandum to the originator. Within five days, the supervisor must also inform the employee as to the actions that will be employed to resolve the opinion. An immediate supervisor, however, has within his or her discretion the ability to determine that a written statement deals with matters excluded from the definition of a *differing professional opinion.* The employee, in turn, can appeal the supervisor's decision to any level of NRC management.

Another safeguard built into the plan, which functions as an objective check on an office director's discretion, is that of the peer review group. At the request of the originator or the immediate supervisor, the differing professional opinion is presented to an impartial peer review group for evaluation, review and comment. It is the office director's responsibility to ensure that members of this group are specifically selected for their impartiality and professional competence in the areas discussed in the differing professional opinion.

The NRC has instituted two alternative channels for expressing differing professional opinions: an open door policy and the Advisory Committee on Reactor Safeguards (ACRS). The latter can be used if the differences relate to a nuclear safety issue. These options allow the originator to select the individual manager to whom the differing professional opinion will be submitted. In addition, each provides for the submission of anonymous statements. If the employee wishes to remain anonymous but desires to have his or her views known as a differing professional opinion, the employee must submit an unsigned statement and forward it to the manager or member of the ACRS contacted via the open door. The manager then forwards the anonymous statement to the office director having programmatic responsibility for issues addressed in the statement. The manager relays to the originator both an acknowledgment of receipt and all reports concerning the resolution of the opinion.

A differing professional opinion is considered resolved by the NRC under five possible conditions: (1) the NRC management adopts the views expressed in the statement; (2) the NRC management adopts some of the views expressed and informs the originator of the reasons for not adopting the remainder; (3) evaluation of the differing professional opinion fails to justify modification of a management decision, policy or practice; (4) the responsible office director determines that the statement does not warrant a detailed evaluation; or (5) the originator withdraws his or her differing professional opinion. The written statement by the employee, along with the response of NRC management, is subsequently placed in the NRC's Public Document Room.

If dissatisfied, the employee may appeal the resolution of his or her differing professional opinion to any higher level of NRC management, including a commissioner or the commission. Furthermore, the appeal may be forwarded through the ACRS, if the opinion concerns matters of public safety, with a request that the ACRS comment on the potential safety implications. One final option available to an employee who is displeased with the results of his or her appeal is to pursue the matter further via the open door policy of the ACRS as appropriate.

No NRC employee is to be retaliated against as a result of submitting a differing professional opinion or lodging a subsequent appeal. The NRC revised its definition of *retaliation:* "retaliation consists of injurious actions taken against the originator of a differing professional opinion in which a *motivating factor* for such actions derived from the submission of a differing professional opinion." This means that the NRC must prove that the adverse action would have occurred even if the dissident had never filed a differing professional opinion.

Eight differing opinions were submitted during the first year the procedures were in effect, and all eight, according to the NRC, were resolved. At present the Office of Management and Program Analysis is in the process of reviewing these procedures.

THE AVCO-EVERETT RESEARCH LABORATORY

In the early 1950s the U.S. Government was becoming increasingly concerned with establishing military supremacy over the Soviet Union. As a result Congress was willing to commit money to develop new weapons. It was also a time when the Air Force was having problems with its new weapon, the intercontinental ballistic missile (ICBM). Dr. Arthur Kantrowitz, a brilliant young professor of gas dynamics at Cornell, was certain that shock tubes, long straight pieces of heavy tubing through which a mixture of gases was pushed at high speeds, could be used to simulate ICBM high-speed flight phenomena. In December 1954, Avco Manufacturing Company received a letter of intent from the Air Force, the contractual basis upon which Avco-Everett Research Laboratory (AERL) was organized and began its work in missile reentry physics. Kantrowitz, the new laboratory director, contacted several highly regarded technical people, and within a few days the group began work on the reentry problems, using the facilities at Cornell University. At the end of six months, the solution to the reentry problem was achieved, although Kantrowitz realized that much research remained to be accomplished. In 1955 the group moved into a new laboratory in Everett, Massachusetts, and the lab was made a separate division of the Avco Corporation. Kantrowitz, in addition to being the lab director, was also a vice-president and director of the Avco Corporation. He had insisted on such a division.

The AERL, now a wholly owned subsidiary of the Avco Corporation, principally conducts high technology research and development under contract to the U.S. government, primarily the Departments of Defense and Energy. It also sponsors development of new technologies that may have potential government or commercial applications and converts existing technologies to commercial use. It is internationally recognized in the field of gas dynamics and specializes in high-power industrial lasers, electrooptical sensing systems and energy technology, particularly its coal gasification system and its magnetohydrodynamics (MHD) activities, both of which offer cleaner and more efficient means of using coal to produce electric power.

The achievements of the laboratory have resulted largely from its ability to conduct interdisciplinary research. Four research committees, which cover certain elements of physical gas dynamics and radation physics, make up the scientific core of the laboratory. Under the leadership of its chairman, each research committee creates an in-depth scientific forum for those laboratory activities that fall under its purview. Research scientists are not only permitted but expected to communicate their thoughts and ideas freely at all stages of their work. The necessary cross-fertilization of ideas is further stimulated by open research committee meetings. which engender appraisal and criticism of scientific research programs under way at the laboratory.

The AERL also has research program offices motivated toward the achievement of specific goals, particularly in areas such as reentry physics, biomedical engineering, commercial lasers, high-power laser technology, and MHD power generation. Each research program office, headed by a vice president, provides an interdisciplinary technical forum for the research components falling within its respective programmatic area, and has overall responsibility and authority for performance, as well as for the general planning and development of funding for that area.

Several additional factors enter into the AERL's notable success. First, their recruiting and hiring practices are quite stringent. Because the lab is similar to that of a university, individual responsibility and initative are highly valued. Candidates for employment at the Ph.D. level are more often than not recommended by staff members and invited to conduct a seminar before a number of the scientific staff. Written reviews are then collected and, assuming they are favorable, an offer is made to the applicant for employment. Aside from an individual's technical accomplishments, the AERL management evaluates a person's ability to develop working relationships with his or her peers, his or her ability to communicate, and whether the person is able to withstand professional criticism. Second, there is not a high turnover rate at the AERL. Employees enjoy a tremendous amount of discretion and freedom in regard to their tasks. Decisions affecting their work and the work of the lab are made by informal consensus rather than by a rigid authority structure. Third, to facilitate the flow of information, to ensure that criticism is constructive, and to minimize wasted effort, the communication networks receive strong emphasis. Scientists regularly give presentations designed to stimulate discussion, debate, and disagreement. This process of peer review has proved to be successful and effective at the AERL: A scientist's work is criticized on technical grounds and personal references are avoided. Fourth, the AERL relies heavily on informal working arrangements and relationships. Research committee meetings are open to anyone to attend, and only to the extent that a scientist identifies with an area covered by a committee is he or she identified with any particular committee. This flexibilitiy of roles allows a scientist to be an atomic physicist in one situation and a budget analyst in another.

All these factors culminate in open face-to-face interactions. Conflicts are addressed on a daily basis in a variety of fashions. Informal consultations occur during "ad hoc corridor" meetings, research committee meetings, technical review meetings, program office meetings, or during the presentations discussed above. Two other mechanisms are employed on a routine basis for resolving technical disagreements: utilization of in-house consultants and external consultants.

Many scientists at the AERL are internationally known in their field and are frequently called upon to offer advice on the best way to proceed with a goal or perform a specific task. While director of the lab, Kantrowitz served as one of the many in-house consultants and was active in helping to resolve numerous disputes.

Additionally, external consultants, about 80 in number, are available to lend their expertise to the scientists at the AERL, review programs, and offer summary criticisms. The advice of the consultants is not binding; scientists are free to disregard it. This freedom is due to the fact that, as one research committee chairman stated, "The consultant coming in here is not particularly better informed or more competent than the scientist(s) who requested him; it's more a meeting of equals than a technical guru with his acolytes."

For more routine personnel matters the AERL has an Announced Complaint Procedure and an Open Door Policy. The former procedure allows anyone with a complaint or some issue or matter that he or she wishes to be known to go through, first, their superior, then the Personnel Department, and up through the chain of command to the chief executive officer (CEO). The latter procedure allows someone to completely bypass that system and go directly to the CEO.

As a result no one can complain that they do not have a forum in which to air important technical issues or air grievances.

CONCLUSION

Sometimes employees feel that they must go outside the organization in order to resolve dissenting opinions. What these three organizations show is that whistleblowing is not always necessary. It is possible to develop mechanisms within the organization that will give professionals a fair chance to air their differences. Whether these mechanisms are located in one individual, a system of appeals or an atmosphere of collegiality, they can help people to resolve their differences amicably, swiftly, and effectively.

PART TWO
CASE
STUDIES

THREE
CONSULTANTS AND
CONSULTATION

THE LABORATORY

Marco-Nevitt Research Laboratory is recognized as one of the top research laboratories in the world. It currently rests on a 200-acre site in the rolling hills of Palo Alto, California, and is composed of several modern structures located in a parklike setting. The scientists working at Marco-Nevitt are considered tops in their fields: many have won international awards for research in such diverse areas as military defense, energy, and medical technology.

Marco-Nevitt's success story is directly related to the charismatic nature of its founder, Stanley Michelson. Back in the early 1950s, before Marco-Nevitt existed, Michelson was recognized as a brilliant scientist and theoretician by his colleagues at Stanford University. It was by chance that he met Roger Jacobs at a faculty luncheon one day in April 1953. Jacobs was one of the rising young executives at Axel Corporation, a firm recognized as a national leader in the manufacture of appliances. He had been invited to be a guest speaker at the faculty luncheon that afternoon and his talk, "The New Alliance between Education and Business," was a most interesting one for Dr. Michelson. After the talk, Michelson and Jacobs continued to debate the issue long into the afternoon. Over the next few months the two became close friends. They shared their concerns about their professions. Jacobs mentioned how Axel was slipping from its number one position in appliance manufacture and was in need of a new direction. Michelson revealed his dissatisfaction with the ivory tower attitude of his colleagues at Stanford. He was ready for a more active career.

Recently, Michelson had been reading about the continuing problems the air force was having with its new weapon, the intercontinental ballistic missile (ICBM). The cold war was on, and national defense was a major issue. With his solid background in aerodynamics engineering, Michelson decided to embark on a detailed investigation of the ICBM problem. After months of study he came to the conclusion that there was a way of simulating an ICBM high-speed test flight using prototype models rather than relying on field tests of the real thing. Currently, this possibility was being totally neglected. He shared his thoughts with Roger Jacobs one evening over cocktails.

Jacobs listened with enthusiasm as Michelson described, in layman's terms, the rationale for his conclusion. He realized that the Department of Defense was investing hundreds of millions of dollars in a wide range of projects and that this stood a good chance of being funded, especially if it were channeled through a recognized corporation such as Axel. This might be the kind of new direction Axel needed. Jacobs brought the suggestion to his superior, whose response was encouraging. Axel was ready to pursue new directions, and contracts with the Defense Department seemed a most attractive possibility at this time.

Over the next several months Jacobs and Michelson collaborated on a plan to develop the Missile Test Program. Early in 1954 the air force granted them a $110 million contract and Marco-Nevitt Research Laboratory was set up under the auspices of Axel Corporation to pursue the mission, with Michelson as director.

The laboratory began with 50 employees and over the next 25 years grew to over 700. Under Michelson's charismatic leadership, Marco-Nevitt moved to the forefront in research and development. Success on the ICBM project led to new proposals and contracts. Half of the staff at Marco-Nevitt are now professional scientists and engineers, with about 200 currently holding advanced degrees. Over $40 million a year is required to support its current size.

Michelson had to shift the directions of the laboratory over the last several years from pure research toward the production of hardware. Economically tight times were forcing many research laboratories in this direction. Michelson was successful in negotiating this shift owing to his effectiveness in creating a positive and supportive climate at Marco-Nevitt over the earlier 20 years. He involved his colleagues in all important decisions and although he was a strong leader, he was effective with a nondirective approach.

Marco-Nevitt's competition had become stronger over the years, with new technological breakthroughs occurring continuously and with the government's becoming more discretionary. The lab was now competing with government laboratories, universities, and other research groups throughout the country. Flexibility and the ability to initiate new directions had become the norm. A delicate balance had to be maintained between the concerns of scientific research and the marketability of products. Fortunately, Michelson was gifted with the ability to inspire those working at Marco-Nevitt to maintain such a balance.

He was effective for a number of reasons. First and foremost, he hired only the best scientists in the field. He demanded of them not only scientific rigor but also the capacity to be a team player.

Candidates with doctorates were usually recommended by staff members and invited to give a seminar before several scientists (normally the audiences' specialties coincide with the speaker's). The usual interviews follow with written reviews submitted to the laboratory director for final approval. Sometimes scientists begin by consulting part-time at the lab and gradually work their way into a full-time position.

The atmosphere at Marco-Nevitt might most accurately be characterized as collegial: It was like a university campus. People are casual in their dress and interactions, office doors are almost always open, and individuals are free to come and go as they desire. Michelson involves himself in a number of capacities at Marco-Nevitt. In addition to his role as laboratory director, he acts both as an internal consultant and as a scientist in his own right. Michelson prides himself on keeping up with various projects at the lab and continually amazes his colleagues with his insightful comments at the weekly project meetings. Whether the project concerns atomic physics or aerodynamics, Michelson is sure to have a comment or suggestion.

Differences of opinion or dissent were a way of life at Marco-Nevitt. There were ample forums, however, for such differences to be resolved, and the lab director's door was always open for complaints. Such conflicts, however, were rarely negative and almost always resulted in stimulating the creativity of all involved.

AN ENCOUNTER WITH THE DIRECTOR

The sound of honkey-tonk piano and the smell of freshly cooking pizza filled the air at Jeremy's Pizza Hut. The men at the table were in the middle of their afternoon lunch and were currently placing an order for their third pitcher of beer. Jeremy's was the local hang-out for Dr. Bob Gallagher and his colleagues from Marco-Nevitt. On this particular Friday afternoon, the topic of discourse was Bob's proposal for a study of coal conversion processes.

> Bob: This whole area of coal conversion is ripe for the plucking. Here we are in the middle of an energy crisis and no one in 40 years has gone beyond preliminary research.
>
> Tom: But Bob, this will mean taking you off the current project, and we really can't spare you at this time.
>
> Bob: Look, Tom, I appreciate your concerns, but I know several guys who can stand in for me on the Solar Project. I've been looking into the coal conversion concept for some time now, and I know I've got something that is going to lead to something big.

Gallagher proceeded to elaborate his idea over the next two hours as the group of scientists continued to consume pizza and beer. In 1974 Gallagher had been hired as a research scientist at Marco-Nevitt. His major background was in combustion fluid flow and propulsion, an area in which the laboratory was intensely involved. Prior to coming to Marco-Nevitt, Gallagher had taught at Stanford. Starting in 1969, he began part-time consulting work at the laboratory and had gradually worked himself into a full-time job.

From his prior experience at Marco-Nevitt, Gallagher knew that there were stiff criteria for new projects to be initiated. First of all, a new project must relate to current work underway at the laboratory. Bob saw no problems here since work was already being done on high-temperature gas dynamics. A second criterion required that the end product must advance knowledge concerning the area of technology. No problem here either. Finally, the new project had to be profitable for the company. If Bob's hunches were right, this might be one of the most successful projects the laboratory had yet undertaken.

As the group was walking out to the parking lot, Bob, feeling he had not really convinced the group, turned to Tom and said, "Well, how about it? What do you think I should do at this point?"

Tom was one of the veterans on staff, one of the first scientists hired by Dr. Stanley Michelson. He knew the ins and outs of the organization and had seen many projects born as well as aborted.

> Tom: My bet is that you're not going to get approval. As I said before, you're already involved with the Solar Project, and you

should see it to completion. Yet, Bob, I respect you as a professional, and think you should talk to the "Boss" for further suggestions.

Early the next week, Bob scheduled an appointment with Michelson. He knew that Michelson was open to new ideas and yet exercised considerable caution before initiating new projects. On the day of their meeting, Bob presented a cogent case for coal conversion. Michelson listened carefully and intently, asking questions at various stages of the delivery. He believed in supporting young scientists like Gallagher at appropriate times. Was this the time, however?

> Dr. Michelson: Bob, you've made an impressive case for this project. I have some objections, however, on both technical and department grounds. You're going to have to get much more support from your colleagues and you've got to develop a stronger case to establish its feasibility. I do believe, however, in encouraging young scientists like yourself, and I've decided to give you some release time and a small amount of financial help from my development fund so you can pursue your idea. You just might be successful. Don't hesitate to call me if I can be of further help.

RESOLVING DISAGREEMENTS

Marco-Nevitt is a research and development organization that utilizes five procedures for resolving professional conflicts: (1) formal meetings, (2) unscheduled informal meetings, (3) special meetings with internal consultants, (4) external consultants, and (5) a formal announced complaint procedure.

Formal Meetings

To understand procedures for resolving professional disagreement, an examination of the laboratory structure would help. The laboratory has a series of program offices that oversee contracts and the actual work that goes on within them. Overlying these offices is a research committee system that has a series of chairmen from different fields. A scientist ends up having two bosses, a common feature of matrix-type organizations. There is a form of crosscheck whereby both program content and technical-scientific content are dealt with in two definite forms.

The chief formal mechanism for resolving professional differences is the holding of formal meetings that include internal technical reviews, working group meetings, committee meetings, and program office meetings. At these, issues are raised and explored in an open forum where each side can present its arguments. Brent Jones, research committee chairman for the aerophysics group, comments:

> Professional disagreements [tend to be resolved] . . . by having one or more people stand up and give a presentation on what they are doing . . . [so as to] . . . stimulate discussion, dissension, disagreement and presumably to either get consensus on what should be done next in order to figure out what to do.

Many disagreements are worked out informally with the research committee. One of the basic purposes of its meetings is to provide an occasion for scientists to inform each other of their activities in the laboratory, thus leading to a cross-fertilization of ideas. Michelson comments:

> [Such meetings] allowed others to object to work that was not well done, that would not reflect well on the laboratory . . . it was the chief administrative procedure as far as I was concerned.

If differences between scientists arose, a decision was reached after examining the different sides of the issue and looking for the most logical position to take. Some scientists complained about the number of meetings. As Arnold Jones, vice-president of planning, laments:

> There are just too many meetings! We have a meeting for the research committee, then you have the program office meetings, and then sometimes you will have special working group meetings. Everybody is invited to go to the meetings. I find that I physically can't do it.

Aronson also mentions the opportunity for scientists to raise issues and make complaints.

> The special meetings are held once a month or every six weeks. No scientist or engineer could really complain about not having a place to voice his opinions, at least about technical problems. He is free to go to any meetings he wants, including those that are not his committee.

A scientist may also go directly to his research committee chairman with problems of professional dissent.

Unscheduled Informal Meetings

Several of the administrators at Marco-Nevitt mention the "university, campus-type" atmosphere that prevails. Many disagreements are worked out informally in the hallways or at off-work locations. As Tom Caswell mentions:

> I chose consciously to get out at least once a month with my guys and other people who choose to come along for just a somewhat fluid lunch of beer and pizza. A lot of things tend to come up that would not be brought up in the office laboratory environment. This opens up communications, ideas, and questions that might not otherwise get raised.

Special Meetings with Internal Consultants

Occasionally, special meetings were called by the lab director to work out differences of opinion. As Michelson recalls:

> I would occasionally use technical adversary procedures in setting up teams to work out various options. We might undertake conflicts and work them out competitively and then decide which way we'd go, based on the presentations.

Sometimes problems are worked out by bringing in an independent party to help resolve the dispute. Dr. Smith comments:

> Internally what we do if there is a conflict in the department, and a department manager has a relationship with an independent party, he'll ask to have him brought in to try to resolve it.

There is usually a preference given to having an internal consultant, people known within the organization, who would listen to both sides and then give an independent conclusion or at least help in smoothing out some of the local problems. Scientists were also encouraged to take advantage of the "open-door" policy of the deputy vice-president of administration or the lab director himself if they were not getting fair treatment through other channels.

External Consultants

Marco-Nevitt utilizes external consultants on an active basis and occasionally brings them in to help resolve internal disputes. The company is very close to Stanford, the University of California at Berkeley, the University of Santa Clara, and other universities, so there is never a problem securing qualified consultants. Sandra Elkins, employee relations specialist, comments on the number of consultants used:

> We have probably about 80 consultants on an active basis, coming here anywhere from three to 20 days a year. They impact over a whole technical spectrum...(and) one or two administrative areas, too.

Consultants are brought in either by the interested scientists or by the lab director. A primary criterion for selecting consultants is related to their reputations and professional expertise in a given area. The major role of the external consultant, however, was to act more as a technical adviser than a mediator. The director or scientists had the option of accepting or rejecting the consultant's advice.

Formal Announced Complaint Procedures

Through a formal process complaints are handled in a systematic way. Leonard Johnson, human resources director, comments:

> Anyone with a complaint or simply something that they want aired first goes through their supervisor and on to the personnel department and up through the chain of command to the chief executive officer. It [also] allows someone to completely bypass that system and go directly to the chief executive officer.

Such a procedure is typically used for personal problems since technical problems are worked out in committee meetings or program review meetings.

THE BIRTH OF A SUCCESSFUL PROJECT

Bob Gallagher felt guardedly optimistic as he left Michelson's office. The lab director had conveyed his reservations and yet had supported him by giving him release time and sufficient funds to pursue his project further. Bob decided that he should begin to address the two major concerns Michelson raised: the need for more collegial support and the resolution of technical problems not adequately covered.

Over the next two months, Bob met regularly with his colleagues and noted their concerns. He listened attentively to their criticism and encouragement. Casual lunches at Jeremy's turned into rigorous evaluations of both the past research and the merits of his proposal. Each scientist seemed to take a turn at challenging it. This open exchange of ideas was typical. Ad hoc meetings often served to inform a scientist that he was incorrect in his initial appraisal of a problem or that he was outside the laboratory's goals. At Marco-Nevitt a scientist was free to pursue his or her own interests within his or her own committee team's area, but the scientist's goals had to be congruent with their goals.

Bob proceeded to involve himself more deeply in the field of coal conversion and to develop a more sophisticated understanding of the technical and other problems associated with this process. He began to realize gradually that there was no definitive answer on the scientific feasibility or practical worth of his project. The informal meetings had served to raise issues and questions and had acted as a stimulus for him to delve more deeply into the problems. But if he were going to get his project off the ground, Bob knew he had to schedule a formal presentation at an official meeting of his research project meeting.

After weeks of preparation Bob was ready for the Thursday morning meeting. Bob's presentation was one of several scheduled for that day. His proposal, however, was the major one. The others concerned minor problems and scheduling adjustments.

Bob was unusually nervous that morning because he realized that a number of the laboratory's top scientists were planning on attending the meeting. Michelson was also expected to be present, and so the pressure was on.

The other presentations went quickly, and the audience became silent as Bob mounted the short stage and proceeded to the podium. He noted a smile or two from his two closest friends, which gave him the emotional support he was hoping to get.

Bob: My dear colleagues, Dr. Michelson, and distinguished guests . . .

Bob proceeded to give an eloquent and authoritative presentation that began with an assessment of his preliminary testing of coal gasification and ended up with a delineation of his research proposal. A question period followed, with a number of positive and negative comments offered by those present. A number of questions were raised that Bob could not answer because they required further research on his part. A few scientists in the back of the room had even entangled themselves in a private argument concerning the proposal. The research committee chairman attempted to control the emotional involvement on the part of some of the more vocal adversaries to no avail. Each argument for or against the proposal was countered by a rebuttal.

Eventually, Bob was able to restore order to the meeting, after acknowledging that some of the negative comments might be proven true with further research. He also conceded a point raised by a colleague about an engineering aspect of his gasification system. Bob was ready for this aspect of the meeting and handled it well. He realized that forums such as this were an essential part of Marco-Nevitt's success story. A scientist is expected to be open to criticism and to be receptive to revisions when warranted. Each argument presented, whether pro or con, had to be supported by scientific data, and no personal attack would be permitted. The Marco-Nevitt committee system was designed to guide research at the laboratory, planned or already underway. Final decisions were made by informal consensus rather than by someone in authority.

It was approaching noon, and the meeting had to be brought to a close. Bob realized that no consensus had been reached. Several of the committee members who voiced conflicting opinions approached Bob afterward though to congratulate him on his efforts and offered to discuss the matter further. Bob had no ill feelings, and actually enjoyed the exchange of ideas. He knew he had made a good impression on a number of the distinguished scientists present, including Michelson. He intuitively knew, however, that he needed a much stronger argument if his project was to get off the ground.

Michelson stopped Bob in the hallway after the meeting and suggested they get together over lunch. At the luncheon, Michelson congratulated Bob on his presentation but again reiterated his concerns, especially the financial risks involved. He suggested that Bob also get some more technical advice and advised him to get in touch with Alex Hopkins, one of the Marco-Nevitt's external consultants who was currently doing work at Berkeley in gas dynamics. The following weekend, Bob drove up to Berkeley for an afternoon meeting. After shared greetings the two sat down on Alex's porch overlooking San Francisco Bay with the "city" skyline off in the distance. It was a beautiful May morning with the smell of eucalyptus in the air. Alex brewed some fresh tea, which the two of them sipped while they discussed their organizations. Alex was currently teaching at Berkeley and did a little consulting work on the side. Like Bob, Alex was getting tired of the academic routine and was looking for more full-time work in the consulting area. Bob was encouraging, for he had found the transition rewarding. Working for an organization such as Marco-Nevitt was a very satisfying way of life. With stimulating work and a supportive climate, what more could one ask for?

Their talk eventually got to the topic Bob was most interested in — coal conversion processes. They spent the next two hours sharing thoughts on the subject and Bob decided that Alex was definitely the man to bring in as an outside consultant. As he was heading back home, Bob could not help but be enthused about his project. Alex was competent and knowledgeable in the field. Many of the concerns raised at the project meeting could be handled with Alex's assistance.

Marco-Nevitt regularly uses outside consultants in a number of different areas — especially where technical issues and problems are of interest. There are currently over 80 consultants on call, and Bob knew that Michelson would give his support to inviting Alex to act as a consultant for his proposal.

Over the next several weeks Alex made regular trips to Marco-Nevitt to help Bob out on the various specific technical difficulties that were brought up at the project committee meeting. As time progressed, however, Bob realized that Alex was not in a position to give full support to his proposal. Alex listed his concerns:

> Although I feel that there is great potential in your ideas, Bob, I see three difficulties. First of all, we both realize that there has been little research in this coal gasification area — it's a risky venture. Secondly, I don't really see any new possibilities in the area of high-temperature coal processing. Lastly, even if the process was possible, I don't think it could be made into a profitable venture for the company.

Bob thanked Alex for his support during the preceding weeks. He acknowledged the concerns Alex raised and decided that he had two options. He could table his proposal, in which case he would be admitting that those scientists who voiced contrary opinions were right, or he could pursue the matter further. Bob's instincts told him that the persons who had objected to the project had not really presented a convincing case that he was indeed beyond the state of the field for this technology. He knew he had to exhaust all avenues available to him at Marco-Nevitt before he relinquished his proposal. The possible benefits both to the company and to society at large far outweighed the risks associated with putting more time into the proposal.

Bob decided a meeting with Michelson was the next logical step. The lab director was noted for his technical expertise in a number of different areas and was very helpful in suggesting strategies for overcoming obstacles such as the present one. Bob reviewed the current status of his proposal and listed both positive and negative criticisms. He once more sought the consultations of his colleagues in a variety of informal settings.

Bob nervously fumbled over the last few pages of his notes as he was invited into Michelson's office.

Michelson: Good morning, Bob! How are things going for you these days?

Bob: Just fine, Dr. Michelson. I really appreciate the time you've given me this morning. I want to get your advice on an important issue.

Michelson: Well, go ahead and I'll see what I can offer.

Bob: I'm at a major juncture in the coal conversion process proposal. On the one hand, I see a number of pluses. First of all, the coal gasification process offers a cleaner and more efficient means of producing electric power. Second, using a given amount of fuel, the process can produce twice as much energy as a conventional gas turbine power plant. Third, fuel reserves will last longer. And lastly, pollutant emission for a given amount of power will be reduced.

Michelson: You're right on all counts, Bob. I'm concerned about investing company money into a project that is a long-term effort. It could be years before Marco-Nevitt could expect any profits from this process.

Bob: I realize that, Dr. Michelson. I just don't feel, however, that enough evidence has been brought to disprove my hunches. If I felt for a minute that this project wouldn't pay off, I would drop it in a minute.

Michelson: I'll tell you what, Bob. I want you to work up another presentation for your project committee meeting that takes place in two weeks. I suggest you seek their approval for a pilot project in this area. You should document very carefully your reasons for the proposal and phrase things so that you don't stir up the ire of any of your opponents on that committee. If you gain their support, I'm for you. Good luck!

Bob left the meeting with an ambivalent feeling. He could tell that Michelson was still not convinced. A major concern was the monetary investment issue. The company was under a great deal of pressure recently owing to shrinking government contracts. Michelson, however, had left the door open again for Bob.

The next weekend was a busy one for Bob as he feverishly went over his notes and worked up a new proposal. He had not thought of making a request for a pilot project. Michelson's suggestion might be just the way to get things off the ground. Bob stopped to see Michelson a few days before the project committee meeting for some final advice.

Bob could not believe how easily the meeting went. Unlike the first, he seemed to be in almost total control as he outlined his proposal and documented his rationale. Several questions were raised, but Bob was ready with supportive evidence. The advice Michelson had given him proved invaluable. The committee unanimously agreed to support Bob's proposed pilot study on the coal gasification process. A major requirement was that each stage of the project be submitted for comment and approval by the Research Committee. The project was subject to discontinuation if major problems occurred.

With company money now assured, Bob and several other interested colleagues formed a team to start the project. Over the course of the next year, the team continued to work on the project and successfully overcame obstacles as they arose. The Research Committee was regularly informed of progress and their support continued. Michelson stopped in occasionally to see how things were going and was obviously pleased at the success Bob's team was having.

Like all projects initially funded with company money, the lead scientist is expected to seek alternative funding to support the continuation of the project. During this first year, Gallagher and his associates submitted several grant proposals to different federal agencies and private utility companies. By the end of their second year, on the basis of preliminary findings, they had acquired funding through the Pacific Electric Institute, a group of electric utility companies, and the Department of the Interior's Office of Coal

Research (OCR). From that point they were guaranteed funding and had full support to pursue the area, since they were not relying on company money.

In 1978 Marco-Nevitt established a new office to coordinate its efforts in developing new energy processes based on coal. Over the subsequent four years Gallagher and his associates made promising and innovative breakthroughs in high-temperature coal processing for energy conversion.

RESEARCH AND REWARDS

Who owns the results of Gallagher's research? At one level the answer seems straightforward enough: the scientist himself or those for whom he or she works. But insofar as each scientist has an obligation to share the results of his or her work, one could equally well answer that the results belong to the scientific community.

For scientists who work in private laboratories, these two answers conflict. In what follows we shall explore the sources and possible solutions to this conflict.

Science and Knowledge

The roots of the word science go back to the Latin <u>scio</u> meaning "I know". Contemporary philosophers have argued that for anything to be knowledge it must satisfy three conditions: traditionally these are justified true belief. Furthermore, for a belief to be justified it must pass a test that is objective and repeatable. It is the actual or possible repetition of scientific experiments that provides a safeguard against fraud and error.

Clearly, on this definition of *scientific knowledge*, if the results of a scientist's work never enter into the public domain, they never achieve the status of knowledge in the full sense.

Science and the Advancement of Knowledge

A second reason for the scientist to share his or her data arises from the cumulative quality of the scientific enterprise. Each scientist builds on the work of others. Although, as Thomas Kuhn has argued, there may be a radical shift in scientific paradigms, much of what the scientist does is an elaboration of prior research of others — qualifying hypotheses, advancing new ones, and refining old ones.

When the results of the scientist's work ar
public domain, this cumulative quality to the sci(
undermined. It becomes more difficult to tak(
research and findings of others. Each investigat
vent the wheel continually because he or she d(
has already been invented by others.

Thus, in addition to the nature of scientific knowledge, the
nature of the scientific enterprise requires that the results of the
scientist's work be placed in the public domain.

The Corporate Right to Privacy

According to a considerable body of law that has developed over
the past 100 years, corporations are like people. Just as each person
has a right to privacy, each corporation has a similar right. Provided
they stay within the limits of the law, they have only a limited
obligation to disclose their internal affairs to the public.

This right to privacy, to be appreciated, fully, must be situated
within a capitalist, competitive context. It allows one organization
to advance its interests in a situation where its gains are another's
loss. When people compete in a race, for one to win, others must
lose. When corporations compete for scarce resources — money,
people, and profits — for one to win, others must lose.

The right to privacy keeps the race fair — prevents one
organization from taking unfair advantage of another. It allows
each to carry on its business with minimal scrutiny of its affairs.

Scientists in Industry

A scientist who works for a corporation is placed in a difficult
situation. As a scientist his or her obligation is to share the results
of his or her work. And yet as an employee, he or she must keep
these results within the organization in order to maximize its
benefit for the employer.

Different kinds of solutions are possible to this moral double
bind. On the one hand, one could simply assert that one's obligation as a scientist takes precedence: Everything a scientist does
would be made publicly available. Or one could assert the para-
mount importance of the organization: Nothing a scientist does
would be shared. Alternatively, one could seek out a middle
ground, a compromise: The results will be shared but in a limited
way.

rco-Nevitt Scientists

The scientists who work for Marco-Nevitt have gone for this compromise. They have tried to develop a system that provides for the sharing of the results of their research, subject to certain restrictions.

The primary vehicle for sharing the results of scientific research within the scientific community is the scientific journal. The results of research can be reported to their peers by publishing articles on it.

Before an article is published at Marco-Nevitt, it is subject to an internal review. In part this mechanism provides a quality control that ensures that the reputation of the Marco-Nevitt scientist is not damaged by faulty research reporting. Since scientific journals provide for refereeing, this procedure is somewhat redundant. But it can serve a second purpose, that is — censorship: research that Marco-Nevitt does not want publicly disseminated can be prohibited from publication.

In practice this seldom happens. Generally, every article submitted to the publication committee is (eventually) published — if it is publishable and worth publishing.

Science and Censorship at Marco-Nevitt

There are several reasons why very little is held back at Marco-Nevitt. First, most of the research that is being reported is pure science, which is not likely to tie into company profits in that form. It is only applied science that is likely to be so immediately useful that it would affect company profits. Second, much of the research at Marco-Nevitt is government sponsored. Since the government is the agent of the public, the public has a greater right to the results of this research. Moreover, one of the measures of the quality of government-sponsored research is the number of publications it yields. Accordingly, it is in Marco-Nevitt's interest to generate as many products of this research as possible. A third reason is the high professional standards among Marco-Nevitt employees. Their commitment to the scientific community is strong and as professionals they would do their best to honor that commitment.

GUIDE QUESTIONS

1. From an organizational point of view, does an informal organizational structure have any drawbacks?

2. Why do you think Marco-Nevitt is successful in resolving professional disagreements?
3. Can you think of a situation where this consultation process would not work?
4. If you were Gallagher, would you have given up?
5. Is it reasonable to provide funds for a project that you reasonably believe will not succeed?
6. What would you do if you were Bob Gallagher and had been refused permission to publish your findings?

SUGGESTED READINGS

Bogen, Kenneth T. "Managing Technical Dissent in Private Industry: Social and Corporate Strategies for Dealing with the Whistle-blowing Professional." *Industrial and Labor Relations Forum* 13 (1979): 1 3–32.

Federation of American Scientists. "New Ethical Problems Raised by Data Suppression." *Federation of American Scientists Professional Bulletin* 2 (November 1974): 1 1–6.

Mozur, Allan. *The Dynamics of Technical Controversy.* Communications Press, 1981.

Nelkin, Dorothy. *Controversy: Politics of Technical Decisions.* Beverly Hills, CA.: Sage, 1979.

Primack, Joel, and Frank von Hipple. *Advice and Consent.* New York: Basic Books, 1974

Reagan, Charles E. *Ethics for Scientific Researchers.* Springfield, Ill.: Charles E. Thomas, 1971.

Rescher, Nicholas. *Unpopular Essays on Technological Progress.* Pittsburgh: University of Pittsburgh Press, 1980.

Sergerstedt, Torgny, ed. *Ethics for Science Policy.* Oxford: Pergamon Press, 1979.

Stanley, John D. "Dissent in Organizations." *Academy of Management Review* 6 (January 1981):1 13–19.

Weart, Spencer. *Scientists in Power.* Oxford: Pergamon Press, 1979.

Weinberg, Alvin M. "The Many Dimensions of Scientific Responsibility." *Bulletin of the Atomic Scientists,* 32 (November 1976): 21–24.

FOUR
FIGHTING A STATE BUREAUCRACY THROUGH COMMUNITY GROUPS

THE ENVIRONMENTAL PROTECTION DEPARTMENT (EPD)

The dawn of the 1970s was marked by a new awareness of the environment and the adverse effects of technology and science on it. The "earth day" activism that followed helped pass tough new environmental legislation. The Environmental Protection Department (EPD) was established in the state of Washington by the governor's office in 1971 in response. With its 2,500 employees and $55 million budget, the EPD was charged with administering and enforcing the state environmental protection laws. To provide a comprehensive approach to the management of the state's natural resources and the control of all types of pollution, the state was divided into six regions. Regionalization, however, created special problems.

First, there was the problem of disparity. Regional directors set their own priorities on how and when to implement a policy or enforce a regulation. This discretion was based on an assumption that complete authority to implement the directives of the Commissioner should be given to each regional director and his or her technical staff. The directives were issued in the form of general policies set by the Central Office. General Counsel W. James Boyd pointed out:

> Different regions performed at different levels in getting these things [directives] accomplished, which indicates that in reality, there was a great deal of discretion even when policy was set.

Each region thus had the freedom to develop its own task, thereby creating, in effect, six separate environmental protection departments.

The second problem was inherent in the structure of the organizational hierarchy. Supervisory control over field staff was ambiguous. For example, the program supervisors for water pollution control, air pollution control, and solid waste were housed in the regional offices and yet reported to both the regional directors and their respective program directors at the Seattle Central Office. This dual reporting system constituted an indirect chain of command to the Commissioner. The regional directors, on the other hand, reported to the Commissioner or the first deputy commissioner, depending on the Commissioner's desires. The program directors were expected to serve in more or less an advisory capacity. The nature of this ambiguity is reflected in a comment by a regional director, Peter Scranton:

> I think sometimes the Program Directors felt that they were in charge of what went on out in the field. There was a little, I don't want to use the word "friction," but it may be a philosophical difference, as to who is making the decisions in the field.

In any matrix organization there is no direct line control over field staff. Program directors at the Central Office often had to rely on persuasion to ensure that their own work was placed high enough on the region's priority list to meet minimum program requirements. Conflicts frequently arose not only between regional directors and the central office but between regional directors and their own staff over how to proceed with a task. Field staff were inclined to be more responsive to the wishes of the Central Office than to the particular needs and priorities of the regional directors because their career ladder and promotional opportunities were through the program divisions rather than the regional structure. This division of power meant that the regional director was not always informed and did not always participate in establishing policy and priorities for the programs that he had to undertake in his region.

THE CHEMICAL WASTE PROBLEM

A crisis arose because the state of Oregon had been accumulating pesticides for a number of years. By 1976 it faced a disposal crisis. The chemicals could not be ignored any longer, and an out-of-state disposal site had to be found.

Messages flew between the Portland office and the Seattle Central Office. Although the procedural hierarchy required that Scranton be privy to all decisions affecting his area in Spokane, he knew nothing about the impending crisis. A joint decision was reached by the offices (without Scranton's input) to ship the chemicals to Spokane where they were to be buried at the site of a chemical disposal firm called Wasteco Disposal, Inc.

The day before the scheduled date of arrival in Spokane, Scranton was alerted by an Associated Press wire that the waste was en route. When it reached his area, he immediately impounded it.

Scranton had been professionally trained as a civil engineer with 30 years of experience. Prior to serving as director, he occupied the position of regional director from 1970 to 1975. He was a scrappy individual, and he believed in protecting the environment at all costs.

Scranton called Commissioner Jim Davis at the Central Office to discuss the situation:

> Jim, I'm calling to let you know that I've impounded that shipment of chemicals from Oregon. The inorganic chemicals can be broken down and placed in the secure landfill since it has an impervious clay membrane which will prevent any leaching problem. The organic materials, however, can't be broken down and we've got to ship them back to Oregon.

Jim Davis replied:

> I'm sorry, Pete, but we've already arranged with the Spokane branch of Wasteco to bury all the chemicals there — both organic and inorganic. They've assured me that there won't be any problems with it.

Scranton was fuming, because he firmly believed that his decision was the only way that the environment would be protected from possible leakage. His assessment was based on sound engineering practices. He knew, however, that Davis and the Central Office were being pressured to help a neighboring state in trouble and Wasteco was the means.

At this point a brief description of Wasteco Disposal, Inc., is appropriate. Unlike county landfills, this private firm derived its profits from storing waste material — the more waste, the better. For several years a senior executive of Wasteco worked closely with the EPD Commissioner on writing environmental conservation law. No money or favors are known to have been exchanged between them. However, campaign records indicated that the firm contributed $5,000 to the gubernatorial election shortly after the EPD was established, and a few months later Wasteco guaranteed a $25,000 loan on behalf of the governor.

Over the next few months numerous meetings were held between Scranton, the Central Office people, and various members of the Boston and Spokane offices. Opposition and confrontation became the rule. Scranton stood firm in his position, but the Commissioner and director of solid waste continued to oppose him. They did not accept his recommendations and, since the waste was already in Spokane, they believed that it may as well stay there.

Clearly, the EPD wanted to keep this dispute out of the public arena. Nevertheless, the Sierra Club got wind of it. A group of students had been collecting data from industrial waste sites in the Spokane region for several months as part of a field study on environmental hazards. This group often reported its findings to the Sierra Club, which occasionally applied pressure on the EPD, various agencies, and politicians to remedy potentially dangerous situations.

On hearing about the impending crisis, Evelyn Fullerton, a leading activist of the club, called a special meeting of the community in which she voiced her concern and called for immediate action.

THE SIERRA CLUB

By this time Scranton felt boxed in. There was no question in his mind that his original decision was correct. He adamantly stated and restated his position to the Commissioner, the program people, and the Portland office. Additionally, he tried to solicit support from his own staff, but they did not want to get involved. It seemed that the harder he pushed, the further they retreated. He and the "others" became adversaries. In his words: "I've said 'no', even though it took a fight to make the 'no' stick. I never did get along with these bureaucrats."

Scranton was no stranger to departmental strife and faced a number of difficulties owing to his tough stands on environmental issues, which often got in the way of getting departmental work done. Two years earlier he had irked his superiors by tying up his entire staff of researchers for a year in a major lawsuit against a local industrial plant. The plant was accused of failing to meet state emission standards. (It was well known that Scranton maintained a tough environmental stand and did not trust industry in the county.) The courts had decided in his favor. Enforcement of the court's decision, however, never took place, largely because of the economic difficulties experienced at that time by local industry, who launched a mass public relations campaign claiming an "emergency" situation threatening their economic survival. Local layoffs were occurring and a nonenforcement sentiment prevailed in the county. During this time Scranton's office was experiencing a notable decline in productivity. As Cecil Spellman, assistant director of the Office of Programming, claimed:

> The work wasn't being done ... There wasn't any production from that office ... in terms of reports, inspections, permits, anything ... We weren't getting any cooperation from the county that we expected, and just simply, the work wasn't being delivered in any category.

Scranton's superiors were also unhappy about his abrasive managerial style, which provoked complaints from people he was supervising or working with. Alex Mason, a regional attorney, commented:

> Scranton had a style unto his own. ... If everything went right, you'd never see or hear him. ... He would review everything (mail, case referrals, etc.) ... and as long as things went smoothly, you never heard from him. ... But, should the slightest thing go wrong or anything happen, all hell broke loose. ... He generally took it out on the regional engineer, Adam Johnson. .. You could hear Scranton screaming at the top of his lungs at poor Mr. Johnson, chastising him for having done something wrong — and I mean literally screaming.

Another incident that earned Scranton further disapproval from his superiors involved the development of a game preserve and hunting reservation near a housing complex. The residents were livid about this and vociferously objected to such an allocation of land. After investigating the situation, Scranton sided with the local community and came out against the developers. His superiors felt that this was a wrong decision and were upset when Scranton came out with a public statement on the matter. No internal mechanisms, however, were available whereby opposing views could be voiced and reconciled within the organization. The EPD, still an infant agency, had not yet implemented any arbitration procedures. So even though he was a "tough enforcer" (in his own words), he got no support, and eventually the game preserve went through in spite of his resistance.

Scranton believed that this waste disposal problem was a do-or-die situation for him, and he was bound and determined not to allow it to go on without a real fight. Again he attempted to resolve the matter by going to his superiors, but once more met stiff resistance. He then realized that it was time to reevaluate his position and come up with some options. Since he was the sole opponent of the waste disposal plan in the department, the simplest solution would be to refrain from criticism and allow the project to proceed as originally conceived. Knowing that his position was right but lacking the power to enforce it, he realized that it was fruitless to continue to protest within the organizational hierarchy.

He needed additional support in the form of pressure that could be brought to bear on his organization. He had no political clout, press connections, or other influential contacts, but he did have a good rapport with the community and its environmental groups. He often kept local environmental and citizens' groups informed about special problems and issues and encouraged them to take an active part in various public hearings.

That evening Scranton called Evelyn Fullerton of the Sierra Club.

Pete: Hello, Evelyn? This is Pete Scranton.

Evelyn: Why, hello, Pete! How are things for you these days?

Pete: Typical, Evelyn, typical. I've run into a dead end down at the department concerning a serious problem.

Evelyn: Is there any way I can help?

Pete: I'm not sure, Evelyn. But maybe you can.

Evelyn: Well, please go on, Pete. What's up?

Pete: The department has given an OK for Wasteco Disposal Co. to store a shipment of chemicals from Oregon at their local land-fill. The problem's not with the organic chemicals that can be broken down and controlled: it's the damn inorganic ones I'm afraid of. There's a good possibility of them leaching into the surrounding area if the inorganic chemicals are not removed.

Evelyn: Don't they know that? What's wrong with the people in your department?

Pete: It's the same old story, Evelyn — political expediency overrides public safety. I've run into a brick wall down here and so I'm turning to you for help. Remember, no names. I don't want to get tangled up with headlines and accusations. It's in your hands. Be assured, however, that I'll supply any information you need.

Evelyn: Don't worry, Pete. I'll get on top of this right away and be in touch with you again soon.

Fullerton called a special meeting of the Sierra Club at which a committee was formed to collect supporting data, disseminate publicity about the incident, and arrange for a public hearing. Commissioner Davis, however, refused to grant the hearing, saying:

This is a routine matter. We're handling things through proper procedures, and there is no need to panic. The public is being protected.

Meanwhile, Fullerton contacted the students who had been reporting to the club and asked that they concentrate on the case at hand. They returned with samples for analysis. Fullerton sent the samples to the Health Department but never received reports. When she called to check on their status, the department told her the samples had been lost!

Fullerton and the members of the Sierra Club special committee decided that it was time to get the matter out in the open. They called another meeting, inviting the public and the press. The *Spokane Messenger* gave second-section coverage to the meeting on the next day, July 19, 1976. The headlines read:

ENVIRONMENTALIST CLAIMS DANGER AT LOCAL LANDFILL

UPI. Dr. Evelyn Fullerton addressed a special meeting of the local Sierra Club claiming a dangerous condition existed at Wasteco's Disposal Co.'s Alton Road Landfill in Spokane County. Fullerton claimed that the State Environmental Protection Department had given an approval for Wasteco to permanently store a shipment of toxic chemicals from Portland, Oregon at their local site. Fullerton asserted that several studies had shown that storage of such chemicals could lead to increased miscarriages, birth defects, and respiratory illnesses for people living in the surrounding area. Fullerton and members of the Sierra Club are actively seeking a public hearing on this matter.

The local television news broadcast a three-minute interview with Fullerton the next day. Following it, a second request for a public hearing was granted.

Through his liaison with Fullerton, Scranton helped the Sierra Club amass supporting evidence for their position. Daily contacts were maintained so that any new developments could be readily communicated. Scranton informed Fullerton of the weak points in the Central Office argument and identified the points on which he had been unable to win. At the hearing Fullerton and her associates testified as to the environmental damages that might ensue as a result of the chemical storage.

Ultimately, a compromise decision was reached in which the inorganic chemicals were buried in a secure landfill in Spokane and the organic chemicals were shipped to an "ordinary" landfill in California. The residents surrounding the California dumpsite subsequently sued the landfill owners, who were later ordered to remove the chemicals.

EPILOGUE

One month after the disposal, Commissioner Davis offered Scranton another job, at a lower level, as regional engineer. Scranton resigned. He now works in the California Environmental Department.

Commissioner Davis felt that he had made a number of sincere attempts to discuss the department's problems with Scranton and work out a mutually satisfactory resolution of the difficulties:

> Peter was a fairly well liked, admired, and respected person. He's been a career employee and has been a long and faithful contributor to the department. I would rate his environmental stand and his interpretation of my policy as being very good. I regretfully had to replace him, for it was the most expedient and effective alternative I had, given the circumstances of his managerial weaknesses.

W. James Boyd, regional attorney, agreed:

> We felt we needed to restructure, that we needed somebody out there who had considerable knowledge of toxic problems . . . so we felt Marconi (Scranton's replacement) would be better for the job. . . He would deal well with the community and would be able to actually carry out some of these things that we knew had to be done. It was unfortunate, probably, the way it was handled . . . and yet there was no easy way to replace somebody.

Fullerton subsequently experienced a variety of problems. She sent more "hot" landfill samples to the Health Department for analysis that were routinely lost. She feels that there has been a deterioration of the relationship between local environmental groups and EDP:

> While Peter was regional director, local environmentalists had a real friend in office. . . Since his departure, such relations do not exist with the present administration.

When she submitted a routine research grant application to the state EDP, it was withdrawn without her knowledge. In 1982 her property was reassessed and her taxes increased. She still actively works with the Spokane Chapter of the Sierra Club, but gets discouraged. She is seriously tempted to accept a teaching offer in California.

MORAL ISSUES

Scranton's case poses several moral problems: selective enforcement, equity, use of community activists, tacit deception, and anonymous whistleblowing.

Selective Enforcement

Pete Scranton likes to keep it simple and shies away from the complexities of political entanglements. He sets his sights on what he thinks is right and goes after it. He is quite aware that conflicts arise because people follow different policies, but he does not recognize that policies are people — moved by a wide variety of feelings, interests, and perceptions. He therefore discounts the reactions of others and acts simply out of the conviction that what he is doing is right.

One major difficulty in his kind of job is selective enforcement. Just as a police officer does not ticket all traffic violators, arrest all trespassers, or charge all violent husbands, environmental officers do not enforce all government regulations: they are selective, they choose on one occasion to enforce a regulation but to disregard it on others.

For Peter Scranton, however, such differential treatment is anathema. He believes that a law is a law, and for that reason alone it must be enforced. Accordingly, he has developed a reputation as one of the toughest enforcers in the field. His philosophy, attractive for its simplicity, is for that very reason impractical. As Immanuel

Kant asserted, and Peter Scranton was forced to concede, "Ought implies can." You cannot reasonably find fault with people for failing to do something they cannot do. Similarly, some companies cannot adhere strictly to regulations governing pollution. They may lack the personnel, the technology, or the finances to implement all the required safety precautions or disposal processes that compliance requires.

In the face of these shortcomings, Peter Scranton is willing to take one step beyond his principle of strict enforcement. The bureaucrat enters: he sits down with the company, works out a schedule, and gives them time to implement it. Ostensibly, this concession is as much of a compromise as Peter Scranton is willing to make. He will not adjust the goal, but he will adjust the speed with which it is pursued.

Unfortunately, he lacks full authority, and others who have regulatory authority are moved by other considerations — primarily expediency, as he sees it. Lower standards are acceptable to them because, in Scranton's view, they are shortsighted — more concerned with doing people a favor or getting along with them than protecting the health and safety of the public.

What makes Scranton different? Because he cannot deal with the complexity of people's motives, he disregards them. Instead, he prefers to focus on high moral principles and lofty goals with which his cohorts disagree.

Equity

Another difficulty with selective enforcement is equity: if a law or regulation is not to be strictly enforced on every occasion, how do you judge the exceptions? The seriousness of the violations is one factor, as criminologists have recognized, and we have noted the ability of an individual or organization to comply as a second factor.

Peter Scranton's critics appeal to disparity to argue against him. They insist that it is unfair to hold companies to higher standards in one region of the country than another. On this principle of equity, the Environmental Protection Agency argued that strict enforcement was unfair if national standards had not been developed. Only if all companies could be held to a single, uniform standard throughout the nation would strict enforcement of that standard be justified. Since they still were federal agencies developing national standards, strict enforcement had to give way to selective enforcement based on the particular circumstances.

Peter Scranton did not accept their position. He sided with the public, not interests of the private company or the needs of bureaucracies. He believed that their interests had to be protected. If a private petrochemical company was making the public waters unsafe to swim in or drink, it would have to be stopped; and if the EPA had not developed national standards to hold them to, he would enforce the state standards.

In effect, he was creating national standards. The fact that years later they were only partially being adopted, and had not been formulated yet in many cases, would seem to prove his point.

Use of Community Activists

Peter Scranton worked through community action groups. As a strategy it worked quite well for him. A number of factors enabled him to be effective through them.

First, he was well positioned. He had considerable authority that was largely unsupervised. The Central Office was 240 miles away from him.

Second, he had ample opportunity to meet members of the community. His job naturally placed him in contact with public officials and required regular attendance at town meetings where controversial incidents were discussed.

Third, his assignments themselves required him to weigh several different factors carefully — in effect, to represent several different groups: private industry, a government bureaucracy, and the community at large. What better way to represent the community than to become well acquainted with its vocal members?

Evelyn Fullerton was one of these, and she was the fourth and most important reason for the success of his strategy.

She held a Ph.D. in biology and was a staunch ally of conservationists. Fullerton was also an active member of the Sierra Club with which she identified (despite her lapsed membership) more than with her employer.

Fullerton possessed a rare combination of attributes that made her a capable and willing ally. She had the credentials to assure credibility. Her technical expertise required that she be taken seriously. She had a firm commitment to the environmentalist cause and promoted it steadfastly. Finally, like Scranton, she had sufficient autonomy to act on her conviction without having her decisions threatened by an immediate superior.

She also possessed considerable resources. As the head of a laboratory that employed seven full-time staff, she had a budget of $200,000 annually that she could allocate to priorities of her choice.

Her relationship with the university gave her access to student-volunteers who had ample time, keen interest, and sufficient expertise under her guidance to conduct sophisticated field research.

Peter Scranton opened his doors to her — literally. She and her students were given ready access to his files and could thereby study carefully the government reports that otherwise would never reach the public.

She also had his ear. When he lost a battle with his organization, Scranton was prepared to go outside it — to her. Providing her with information to challenge claims made by public officials or industry representatives at town meetings proved to be an effective check on careless or inaccurate statements. The mere threat of a detailed rebuttal in a public forum from a competent and informed expert restrained both groups from a temptation to which they might otherwise succumb.

Was Peter Scranton wrong to leak information to a community group? Was he using Evelyn Fullerton for his own purposes? She did not think so — or at least, if he was using her, she was a willing instrument of his purposes, for she believed that his heart was in the right place.

Yet the privileges that she and her students enjoyed were questionable. Scranton viewed them as an extension of the right she would be accorded under the Freedom of Information Act. To his colleagues, though, it would have seemed an unwarranted intrusion into the inner workings of the governmental machinery.

Tacit Deception

The central office knew little or nothing of Peter Scranton's relationship to Evelyn Fullerton. He could not conceal it entirely, but he did nothing to publicize it. Rather, he kept it confidential.

Was he lying? He preferred not to talk much about it and refrained almost dogmatically from naming people. To some extent his reticence had a moral justification: he could thereby avoid name-calling and act with integrity. It was also self-serving: by not telling people what he was doing, he never had to lie explicitly about it.

He misled them, nevertheless, by not being perfectly candid. From his perspective he had too many battles to fight, too many just wars to wage to bother much about the means he used to wage them.

Others would not be so charitable. He was a poor sport, a sore loser. He fought his battles within the EPD, and when he lost he should admit defeat. He did not and would not. Too much was at stake to allow any shortsighted bureaucrats to win.

Yet Scranton did accept one restriction on his relationship with community groups: he would never use them to blow the whistle publicly. Indeed, so strongly did he feel this aversion to publicity that he did not enjoy seeing his name in print. He would be happy to talk with people based on an open-door policy but preferred not to mention others by name. When asked directly why he did not openly blow the whistle on some of the wrongdoing he knew about, he replied sincerely that he believed that such an action would be wrong. When he did inadvertently raise a public outcry, he accepted chastisement from his peers and superiors. Clearly, he was conflicted, and preferred to see himself not as a whistleblower at all, not even as an anonymous one.

Did his strategy of blowing the whistle anonymously through community action groups succeed? The results are mixed.

He did succeed in preventing one Oregon company from burying toxic chemicals in an unsecured landfill in his area, even though he had to take on the EPA, head office, and Oregon officials.

He did successfully litigate a case against a Spokane industrial plant for failure to meet state emission standards, with the support of civic groups and with little or no help from the EPD.

In the first case, however, the most he could achieve was "displacement." Just as saturated patrol, strict law enforcement, and aggressive prosecution simply move crime from one community to another, Peter Scranton's action merely moved pollution around. The toxic chemicals were buried in California, and only later did the residents discover the noxious fumes leaking into their air.

In the second case, despite his spectacular court victory, the detailed schedule for compliance that was worked out was never enforced.

Peter Scranton was himself displaced. He was offered a transfer into a less responsible position. He refused and offered his resignation instead. Because he did his job too well, he was not allowed to do it at all. The chemical companies found it cheaper to contribute funds, indirectly, to a governor's campaign in the hope that his victory would enable them to solve their problem. It did!

GUIDE QUESTIONS

1. Do you believe that Scranton should have resigned?
2. Was Scranton successful in your view?

3. What helps to make community groups an effective strategy?
4. Were any other options available to Scranton?
5. Why do you think he wanted to remain anonymous?
6. Why do you think Scranton was not informed about the proposed chemical storage?
7. Does Scranton need additional managerial training? Would it have helped?
8. Do engineers make good managers?

SUGGESTED READINGS

Baum, Robert J., and Albert Flores, eds. *Ethical Problems in Engineering.* Vols. 1 and 2. 2nd ed. Troy, NY: The Center for Study of the Human Dimensions of Science and Technology, 1980.

Decision Making for Regulating Chemicals in the Environment. Washington, DC: National Academy of Sciences, 1975.

"Defeat for Scientific Integrity: Scientists Testify in DDT Hearing." *Business Week,* July 8, 1972, p. 60.

Kardestuncer, Hayrettin, ed., *Social Consequences of Engineering.* San Francisco: Boyd and Frazier, 1979.

Nader, Ralph. "No Protection for Outspoken Scientists." *Physics Today* (July 1973):1 77–78.

Nelkin, Dorothy. *Controversy: Politics of Technical Decisions.* Beverly Hills, CA: Sage, 1979.

Perry, Tekla S. "Knowing How to Blow the Whistle." *IEEE Spectrum* 18 (September 1981): 56–61.

Unger, Stephen. *Controlling Technology.* New York: McGraw-Hill, 1983.

Weil, Vivian, ed., *Beyond Whistleblowing.* Chicago: Illinois Institute of Technology, 1984.

FIVE
PESTICIDES AND
THE PRESS

THE ANNOUNCEMENT

For five years Robert Kelly, an agriculture pesticide research scientist, had been warning his employer, the Virginia Farm and Produce Agency (FPA), that a toxic chemical, nevrin, was dangerous when sprayed on corn fields. Not only did it cause mutations in the crops, but it poisoned those who ate it — cows, chickens, and consumers of dairy products, beef, and poultry. Over the years Kelly had amassed considerable evidence in support of his two allegations. The animal feed contaminated beef and milk and made chickens lay smaller, discolored eggs. Humans who ate the beef, dairy products, poultry, and eggs suffered from intestinal tumors after a latency period of several years.

Kelly was collecting soil samples from the southern part of the state on September 3, 1976. He carefully marked several specimens and sealed them in plastic bags to take to the laboratory for analysis. By early afternoon the sun disappeared behind an overcast sky. After the clouds had broken, Kelly piled his tools and samples into the car to head for shelter — his laboratory.

He turned on the radio to retreat from the storm. Among other news events reported, he heard that a federal Environmental Protection Agency (EPA) scientist had reported that nevrin, a corn pesticide, was accumulating in the food chain, causing human illness. The commissioner of the FPA, when contacted for comments by a reporter, stated: "This nevrin matter is a serious problem. The Department is now undertaking a careful study of the situation and will take appropriate action." In disbelief Kelly turned up the radio's volume. No further details of the report were forthcoming.

Kelly turned it off. The next day the Washington *Post* ran the following headline:

BEEF AND POULTRY CONTAMINATED

During Kelly's five years of trying to alert the FPA to the nevrin situation, the commissioner had never even acknowledged the presence of the pesticide. Now, an *outside* source, a federal employee, had caught his attention and received action! Kelly grumbled:

> Well, son of a bitch! All these years I've been analyzing samples, consulting with other scientists, speaking at meetings — all these years — and from the *outside* the Commissioner hears that nevrin is dangerous. Where the hell do my data go? Is there a black hole in this bureaucracy?

THE EARLY YEARS

Kelly's perspective had changed since his early years at the FPA. The agency had assumed a regulatory posture because in the early years there were frequent confrontations between those who wanted to exploit the land for profit — farmers and chemical manufacturers — and those who wanted to protect it — conservationists and landowners. The agency sat in the middle, attempting to make use of the resources as well as protect the environment. Consequently, inertia and compromise often led to inaction. Bureaucratic bungling and constant opposition had slowly made him a bitter and frustrated man. It is impossible to mark the turning point precisely, but at some time in 1976 he began to figure out the rules for playing political ball with the big boys — the bureaucrats.

When Kelly first started with the FPA in 1970, he admired and respected his superiors. He once commented:

> I think I was somewhat of a different person in the beginning. I would say in the first place, I had a certain awe of commissioners, of people up the line, a feeling that perhaps these people really knew what they were doing. I thought they must have been competent, that they were looking out for the welfare of the agricultural environment.

He often worked long hours on his own time in his small laboratory in Richmond, Virginia, the state's capital. The laboratory, far removed from the political pressures under which most of his department operated, was his home. Kelly was content to confine his responsibilities to analyzing soil samples and crop mutations and leave the decision-making to the senior staff whose judgment he trusted. He believed that management listened to his and other scientists' advice and therefore made informed decisions. Administration, he thought then, was best left to the experts.

During his early years with the FPA, from 1971 to 1976, Kelly became increasingly sensitive to the risks associated with toxic substances. He was especially concerned because crops were becoming more and more dependent on chemical boosters — pesticides and fertilizers. Since their effects on the land were often irreversible, their use needed to be carefully monitored. Scientists and nonscientists alike were becoming increasingly concerned, as evidenced by such publications as Rachel Carson's *Silent Spring*. Ironically, efforts to mold the environment to suit society's needs were sometimes causing more harm than good.

Kelly's preliminary research on pesticides indicated that, before long, corn would be inedible. He was so astounded by the results that he reran the data two more times. Indeed, his first conclusion was correct. One study he conducted with three scientists from another state found that in four out of seven regions in Virginia nevrin levels exceeded the federally established contamination limit for the commercial sale of corn: the highest level found was more than eight times the limit. Kelly began informing his superiors of his findings, hoping to remedy the pollution problems or at least prevent the situation from worsening.

His career prospects at the FPA were bright. In the spring of 1974 he received a promotion to associate research scientist, and in the following year he published three well-received articles. He was also credited with several advances in the development of inexpensive organic fertilizers. Within the scientific community he was gradually gaining a solid reputation.

He was angry that his department did not take his calls for alarm seriously, especially in view of the supporting evidence he had carefully assembled. Gradually, he came to understand, however, that his department was top-heavy in administration, understaffed in research, and ill-equipped to deal with specialized environmental problems. By one estimate, a well-run laboratory needed at least $100,000 per year and three good technicians. His laboratory operated on a budget of $45,000 and was staffed by him and a part-time technician. They were expected to carry out the soil and crop analyses for the entire state of Virginia. To make a more accurate assessment of the extent to which the crops were contaminated by toxicants in the state, he sought additional support — both people and money.

He argued that industries releasing unspecified chemicals under permit must be monitored more closely — that toxicological testing was not only warranted but required. He attempted to make his department aware of his own studies as well as studies done in other states. He forwarded memo after memo through the chain of command with meager results. In all he sent over 100 memos to administrative officials within the FPA hierarchy during the early 1970s, but rarely received a response beyond an acknowledgment.

THE TURNING POINT

Kelly's initiation into the politics of bureaucracies occurred with that radio announcement in late 1976. He heard an EPA scientist publicly warn of the possibility of nevrin contamination and receive an immediate response from the commissioner. In contrast, Kelly's numerous memos had gone unanswered for months — even years. The fact that the commissioner had been alerted to the problem by an outsider disillusioned and frustrated him. Apparently, all his past efforts had been wasted. Yet the icing on the cake was still to come. Ten days after the radio announcement, the new commissioner banned nevrin and issued a press release:

> The corn pesticide, nevrin, will be banned for use on crops pending the results of studies on its impact on the environment.

What had happened to Kelly's own studies? Why did the FPA not respond to them — or use them now? The state agency, designed to deal with agricultural matters, had become a paper-shuffling mammoth: its own employees, including the man in charge, did not know what was going on.

Others in the agency were less cynical. They accepted that priorities differed between management and scientists. Most of the department's resources for studying pollutants were expended on other chemicals. Very little money was left and consequently the nevrin studies were relegated to a back burner. Also, the department was new and in-house conflicts blurred the lines of responsibility among the different divisions of the FPA. The Division of Soil and Crop Analysis was responsible for reporting pollution, whereas the Division of Pesticide Control monitored the effects of chemicals on crops: Kelly's concerns fell unhappily between the two.

The top administrative structure had changed repeatedly during the early 1970s. The first commissioner was a political appointee, an "amateur" who lacked technical credentials. The next incumbent began to address environmental concerns, but left after ten months because of a change in the governor's office. In Kelly's view he accomplished a great deal during his short stay. The next commissioner, considered by some to be politically ambitious, was unpopular. His indifference to daily or routine departmental affairs resulted in a small following among the FPA staff, but his speaking out on the nevrin matter was encouraging to Kelly, even though he was not a scientist and had only a limited understanding of the matter. Kelly learned a valuable lesson: the upper echelon of the FPA was more sensitive to politics than to its own scientific reports.

He began to redefine his role at the FPA. Having lost faith in his superiors' willingness or ability to protect the state's consumers, he made it his personal responsibility to inform not only his superiors but the public in general of his findings. He would no longer be a diligent and unobtrusive laboratory scientist, content to disseminate his data in professional journals — that was not an effective way to bring about change. The FPA machinery responded to political pressure — from the outside — and that was the route he resolved to take from now on.

ONOZINE AND APPLES

His first opportunity arose shortly after the nevrin announcement. In the fall of 1977, while gathering soil and vegetation samples, he learned that extremely high concentrations of another pesticide, onozine, were present in apple orchards — not just in the soil, but in the trees and apples. Onozine was highly toxic to bees, and often killed these important pollinators. It also killed many other insects, both harmful and beneficial ones. Testing on laboratory animals had indicated that it was a carcinogen.

Virginia Chemical Company (VCC) was the sole manufacturer or onozine in the state. The chemical was primarily used as a commercial pesticide, but it was also sold as a fire retardant. Kelly asked a regional engineer elsewhere in the state to pull VCC's permit. He was horrified to find that it was all legal. The FPA had permitted VCC to manufacture and use onozine. In fact, the FPA even endorsed it as "effective in controlling damage to apple groves caused by *Porthetria dispar"*, commonly known as tent caterpillars. It was also inexpensive for the company to produce and for the farmers to buy. The agency placed heavy emphasis on Virginia's agricultural production and aided farmers by allowing them generous use of pesticides and fertilizers — including onozine.

THE RICHMOND CONNECTION

Kelly felt that too much emphasis had been placed on agricultural production and not enough on environmental protection. He once again tried to alert his superiors via internal memos of the contamination threat and urged that the pesticide be banned.

He was worried about the chemical, and it bothered him that his agency had known since 1973 that large amounts of the chemical were present in several apple-growing regions of the state. For several years he had studied onozine's effects on insects, birds, apples, and test animals. He sent reports of each study to Jamison (chief of the Bureau of Agriculture), Day (director of the Division of Soil and Crop Analysis), and the commissioner. He spoke at departmental meetings and published two articles on his findings.

Finally, after once again getting no action, he was ready to try something new. He told the director that he was going to contact the press, the *Richmond Herald*, but his announcement received no response, so he called Hugh Sealey, a well-known reporter in the capital. Sealey, knowing nothing of Kelly or the situation, initially refused to print any story based solely on Kelly's findings, but he hesitantly agreed to run a story if Kelly could provide documentation and corroboration from other reliable sources. So Kelly pulled his laboratory reports, several toxicologists' reviews, pathologists' studies, and two articles he had recently read in professional journals. He again called Sealey, explained that he had gathered all the materials, and said he would deliver the documentation — but asked that he remain anonymous in the article. Sealey, clearly irritated by this request, told Kelly that he could "identify himself or the story would not be printed." He explained that stories have owners and the public has a right to know who they are. After a long pause Kelly acceded. During those few silent seconds his mind fleetingly considered the consequences — pressure, demotion, dismissal — but he stopped himself. Onozine was too dangerous.

About the same time a local reporter learned of the controversy that was brewing and asked for Kelly's comments. With his memos in hand, the scientist accused the FPA of being an active accessory to the destruction of the Virginia environment. The following day his allegations were brought to the attention of both senior management and the public. The *Richmond Herald*'s Tuesday morning headline read:

PESTICIDE CONTROVERSY AT FPA

Anonymity was no longer an option. Directly above the headline Kelly saw a one-by-two-inch photograph of himself. The article described his unsuccessful attempts to inform his superiors and his department's refusal to acknowledge the threat to one of Virginia's major industries.

The press reached scores of people overnight. Telephone lines to the FPA were overloaded all day Tuesday and Wednesday, and hundreds of telegrams and letters were received. Kelly was contacted by NBC News for an interview. He consented: Even though it was his first time on the air he appreciated the attention. All he had to lose was his low profile. He believed now that the more publicity he received, the more his department would be pressured to investigate his allegations. The next time the commissioner saw his name on a memo, he would read it.

Kelly wore his flowered tie and new dark blue suit to the interview. Between his humor and his sincerity it went very well:

Q: Do you feel it is safe to eat the contaminated apples?

A: I wouldn't eat them: I want to stay alive and healthy.

Q: How can you be so certain that this chemical, onozine, is dangerous?

A: I conducted tests in my laboratory for three months on rats and found it positively correlated with cancer. My results have been confirmed by other scientists too.

Q: Is it not your job, as a scientist, to test your hypotheses and leave the policy judgments to others?

A: You're referring to what I call the "soldier syndrome" — don't question your position in the front line. But I went to college in the period of social conscience. Physicists began questioning the atomic bomb and draftees questioned the war. I respected the social obligations one had in various roles — including my professional duty to weigh moral considerations in my work.

Q: Let's get back to onozine. Did you send your results to your superiors?

A: Yes.

Q: What happened?

A: Nothing.

Q: Nothing at all?

A: That's right.

Q: Did you talk to anyone at FPA about your results?

A: Yes, I spoke with John Jamison, chief of the Department's Bureau of Agriculture. He said: "You don't really know what you're talking about. We will read your report and take appropriate action. Trust us — we'll make the decisions. You just do your job!"

Q: Did you talk to anyone else?

A: Yes. I spoke with Philip Day, director of the Division of Soil and Crop Analysis. He said: "There's no problem — don't worry about it."

Q: What do you think is the problem?

A: First, scientists like me are too far removed from top management. We receive no feedback and our studies are "sanitized" by middle-level administrators.

Q: Now that the cat is out of the bag, do you fear reprisals?

A: I was terrified when I initially contacted Sealey of the *Richmond Herald*, but I decided there was no choice — I would not compromise my standards. Now I am determined to push on. I am a civil servant and we all know how difficult it is to get rid of state employees. And, I am a scientist and we are an independent lot:

lot: we have our own data . . . and clout . . . and we are not as prone to administrative politics as many employees.

Q: Do you foresee similar situations in the future?

A: Yes. It's the nature of our business. Industry wants to sell its products and the government wants industry to grow. I believe that many more chemicals will be introduced in the years ahead that will be equally, if not more, dangerous than onozine. As I see it, it's my job to inform the FPA, as well as farmers and the public, about the dangers.

Q: What will you do when that happens?

A: The same thing: I'll tell my story to the press, and to the people. Now a couple of reporters know me and respect my judgment. I have proven I can prove what I say. Furthermore, I think my issues are real "public interest" grabbers and the press is aware of that.

Within a month of the publicity, the recently appointed commissioner announced at a press conference that Virginia Chemical Company could no longer sell onozine as a pesticide because it posed too great a risk to the consumer. Kelly had accomplished through the newspaper story what he had been unable to do in six years of writing memos.

THE PRESS AND SUCCESS

Kelly was indeed successful in using the media. As a whistleblower he got what he was after. In this instance Kelly was concerned that he ensure public safety and inform the FPA and the public at large of potential hazards. His actions resulted in prevention of potential wrongdoing. The Virginia Chemical Company was not allowed to sell the pesticide, and crops and consumers were protected by its absence. Because the wrongdoing was squashed and the information was publicized, individuals were able to avoid becoming victims of the potential danger. Thousands of people read about the dangerous pesticide in the *Richmond Herald* and the local newspaper. The readers could protect themselves by not eating contaminated food. Furthermore, because the pesticide was banned, future crops would be safe to eat.

Another measure of success is policy change. The FPA indeed altered its plans when the Commissioner issued a public statement banning onozine's use as a pesticide.

Kelly, himself, was astounded by the results. In six years he had never received this much attention — about anything. His inital fears quickly subsided when he realized that he had finally gotten action. Like a locksmith, he had cracked the combination.

ATTEMPTED PERSUASION

Although he was never formally told that he could not voice his professional opinions publicly, FPA officials, according to Kelly, attempted to divert his energy from the media and appease him through promises of additional funding for studies. He remembered:

> My first feeling when they talked to me was: "They're going to get me away from talking to the press by making me think that I will get some money." So I wrote these grant proposals and submitted them. Nothing happened. A few months later they said, "They were good proposals, but there's no money this year. We'll give it high priority next year."

Next year, again, there was no money.

The costs associated with protecting the state's land, crops and human health were high for the scientist. Once his superiors realized that he would continue to go outside the FPA hierarchy with his data, they applied subtle pressure — camouflaged as budget cuts and reorganization. His department — formerly a section, albeit a small one — became a unit. With only one assistant per year, he was forced not only to conduct his research but to file his own papers and even clean the lab floors!

But Kelly was proud of his accomplishments. He had played a key role in the agency's decision to ban the pesticide manufactured by Virginia Chemical. Today he is one of Virginia's leading environmental crusaders and frequently contacts the media to inform the public about consumer and environmental dangers. He recently made the following statement to the Virginia Farmers' Association, which was recorded on the "Week in Review" program:

> The growing number of toxins has made farming very complex. We find ourselves in a highly polluted land that has depleted and mismanaged her finite resources. Even the bald eagle, adopted

as the symbol of the United States 200 years ago, is threatened by pesticides and habitat destruction.

All living things require a suitable habitat, but man has been careless with his environment. Highly productive wetlands continue to be used as landfills and housing developments.

The United States is a major agricultural producer, but in 1975 we lost two million acres of farmland. Over a million acres of rural land became urban developments. Since 1955 we have lost more than 50 million acres of farmland.

Because of increased demands on American agriculture, farming has become more intensive. To increase efficiency large areas are devoted to a single crop, but this also increases the crops' susceptibility to diseases. Fertilizers, insecticides and herbicides are being used at an alarming rate, but only one-half of the country's cropland is protected from erosion and 3.5 billion tons of soil are lost annually. The present trend in agriculture decreases wildlife habitat and increases pollution to all life.

The carbamate and organophosphate pesticides need to be more thoroughly studied for their impact on the environment. Since these pesticides can kill soil microfauna and greatly lower insect population, including the majority of insects that are beneficial, we must consider the environmental consequences before allowing their uncurbed use. Most chemicals released into the environment have not received adequate testing and may cause chemical environmental crises similar to DDT and PCB.

If patriotism is allegiance to one's country, then Americans should respect and protect the land's finite resources. To thoughtlessly despoil the nation's resources threatens the health of the nation, its people, and the plants and animals within it. We must reverse this past trend to benefit all living things.

EPILOGUE

Shortly after the above statement to the Virginia Farmer's Association, Kelly's confidence in the security of his position was shaken. A newly developed fertilizer rapidly transformed string beans into "jack-in-the-beanstalks." Kelly, always cautious, ordered a laboratory analysis of the soil and vegetation to determine the effects of the fertilizer. The analysis showed a toxic residue that lingered in the soil. A month later he retested it, hoping that the toxicity would have diminished to a reasonably safe level, but the second laboratory report looked much like the first.

On the basis of both reports he wrote to his superiors warning that the chemical would accumulate and cause the soil to be unusable within a few years. Kelly argued that in the long run preserving the quality of the land outweighed immediate production considerations.

The agency responded three weeks later by limiting his authority to order tests for soil and crop analysis. The memorandum addressed to him allowed such testing only when crops were undersized or diseased and under no other circumstances. His key weapon against agency inertia, laboratory analyses, had been taken away. Without reports he could not confirm, or for that matter disconfirm, his suspicions. Data would be left dangling, inconclusive. The Wednesday morning edition of the *Richmond Herald* told the story:

STATE ENVIRONMENT WARRIOR DENIED KEY WEAPON

GUIDE QUESTIONS

1. What kind of alternative organizational structure would help ensure that scientific data reach the decision makers?
2. Should Kelly's research and all other government-sponsored research be made publicly available?
3. How long should Kelly have waited before "going public"?
4. Would you have waited as long as he did?
5. Should scientists have a voice in policy matters? If so, how would this be achieved?
6. What other options, if any, were available to Kelly?
7. How effective would they have been?
8. Would Kelly have been justified in going to the media without having first attempted to resolve the onozine controversy internally?
9. Sealey, the reporter, initially refused to publish Kelly's findings and demanded independent corroboration. In the future should Kelly be required to substantiate his allegations, independent of his own studies?
10. If Kelly had refused to be identified in the article, should Sealey have reported it anyway? If he had reported it, would he have been justified?

SUGGESTED READINGS

Anderson, Jack. "A Toxic Cover-Up at the EPA." Washington *Post*, May 4, 1982.
Carson, Rachel L. *Silent Spring*. Boston, Mass.: Houghton Mifflin, 1962.
"Tight Screening Plan for EPA Data." *Science*, September 1981.

SIX
POLITICS, PROTEST, AND THE PROFESSIONAL SOCIETY

THE CRISIS

Margaret Clinton was hired as a senior information scientist by the city of Chicago's Municipal Health Planning Council (MHPC) in early 1977. She had 13 years of experience in the data processing field, with 7 years in management positions. Margaret was seen by her earlier supervisor as "extremely diligent" in carrying out her responsibilities, evidencing "loyalty and enthusiasm." Her new job involved reviewing computer projects, evaluating computer programs, undertaking feasibility and cost-benefit analyses, conducting short- and long-range planning for the citywide information system, and doing detailed work on the individual installation plans.

One of the major projects with which Margaret became involved was the development of a new on-line computerized Accounts Payable System (ACPAS), which would be used by city hospital administrators to manage the patients' billing. Over the past few years, the number of forms that needed to be filled out and filed had increased exponentially, and hospital administrators were becoming buried in paperwork. It was hoped that this new computer system would be as successful as another on-line computer system that was operated by the hospitals to monitor the condition of patients in intensive care units. This second project, called PAMOS (Patient Monitoring System), was an emergency on-line monitoring system that immediately notified nursing stations in the hospital if a patient's vital signs became critical. When emergencies occurred, the nearest nursing station was notified at once: it could then quickly send a head nurse to the hospital bed and contact the patient's physician, whose name was called up on the video screen by the computer. It was generally recognized over the years that delays had been significantly reduced by this system and that this inevitably led to patients' lives being saved in critical situations.

Margaret was very impressed with the medical people who were involved in PAMOS: Dr. Ronald MacIntyre, who was in charge, and nurse Sarah Livemore, who actually ran the computer. The three of them had developed a very good working relationship in a short period of time.

As they were working in the computer center one day, a phone call came through, and Sarah picked up the receiver. Margaret stood in amazement as Sarah began to raise her voice and after a few moments became almost hysterical. Sarah slammed down the phone and said:

> We've just been ordered to put the front end of the new system (ACPAS) onto PAMOS.

She and Sarah knew at once what that was going to mean. The concurrent use of the computer facilities with this kind of setup could lead to an overload, thus delaying the response time to PAMOS's patients. If this occurred, nurses and doctors would not be able to respond as quickly to crises, and thus the patients' lives and health would be jeopardized. The ultimate effects could be an increase in the risks of cardiac arrest and possibly death.

Margaret was confused about what she should do in such a situation. She did not want to endanger her new position in the organization by objecting to orders from her boss. On the other hand, she felt an obligation, as a professional scientist responsible for the technical functioning of the new computer system, to protect people's lives.

THE PROFESSIONAL SOCIETY

The Institute of Electrical and Electronics Engineers

She decided that it was time to seek advice from the professional society to which she belonged: the Institute of Electrical and Electronics Engineers (IEEE). The IEEE is the largest engineering society in the world, with almost 200,000 members. Around 1970 it enlarged its scope from a strictly technical society to address questions of professional responsibility and ethics. As a result the IEEE constitution was amended to incorporate these professional concerns.

The Committee on the Social Implications of Technology (CSIT), formed by IEEE in 1971, publishes a newsletter. It put a notice in its newsletter to inform IEEE members that it would support engineers who had been placed in jeopardy as a result of adhering to their code of ethics. Of the 200,000 members, however, only 3,000 subscribed to the newsletter.

The IEEE closely resembles the American Association of University Professors (AAUP). Both organizations apply moral pressure on groups by investigating alleged abuses and publishing reports of wrongdoing, including names.

One controversy provided the major stimulus for establishing a code of ethics. The Member Conduct Committee (MCC) was set up to enforce the code by supporting those who abide by it and later suffer the consequences of their actions. One of the basic principles of the IEEE code of ethics states:

> Engineers shall protect the safety, health and welfare of the public and speak out against abuses in these areas affecting the public interest. (Article IV, item 1)

Some Alternatives

Why did Margaret Clinton choose the IEEE? First, they were a group of her peers — other engineers. At work no other employee was a qualified engineer. Nobody else had the expertise to make an informed decision. Second, Clinton's objections were morally founded and could be justified by citing several sections of the IEEE code of ethics. Third, the Committee on Social Implications of Technology was young and enthusiastic. It was willing to give special attention to this case. Fourth, the committee promised a great deal of support. To apply moral pressure on the industry, Clinton needed the recognition the committee could provide through its affiliated publications.

The most viable alternative was probably the courts, but Clinton did not consider them because she felt that taking one municipal agency to another municipal agency would prove fruitless. Moreover, she did not have the stomach for a legal battle.

Why not the press? She certainly would have captured the public's ear over this potential hospital crisis — patients dying to ease the pangs of bookkeepers! As a shy and somewhat introverted person, however, she hesitated to talk with reporters: she did not possess the flair required to deal with the publicity. Finally, she dared to call the Chicago *Tribune*. The reporter's final words were curt and to the point: "Call me when there's blood!"

Community groups were out of the question. People who blow the whistle through citizen action groups need sophisticated interpersonal skills: they must be able to relate to residents on the streets and in town meetings. Clinton's strengths lay more in her technical knowledge than in her communication skills.

Congress, legislature, and regulatory agencies, all bureaucracies, provided neither expertise nor support. None of these could match the aid or expertise that the IEEE could provide. Only engineers or computer specialists could appreciate her technical concerns.

The Chronology

At the end of May 1977, Clinton, although still an employee, was at her wit's end:

> For a long time I stared at the wall. I didn't know what to do. Then it struck me: I'm not the only person who's been through this. There is somebody who knows about ethics. Richard Boyle, Chairman of IEEE's Working Group on Professional Ethics, had written about the celebrated Bay Area Rapid Transit (BART) case. He would know what to do and could guide me through it.

Richard Boyle, chairman of the IEEE working group on ethics, was a computer specialist at the Illinois Institute of Technology. He and other members of the IEEE group discussed the matter with Margaret. After several lengthy sessions, they came up with a list of suggestions.

First, they advised her to consult with the director of the University of Chicago's computer center. He was a well-known expert who was knowledgeable in the technical issues she raised. Margaret did this, and her concerns were substantiated when the director concurred with her assessment. He felt that the computer system could be degraded if PAMOS and ACPAS were connected as planned.

Next, the IEEE group suggested that Margaret discuss the situation with her boss. They helped her draft a memo to him that listed the primary concerns being raised, along with a recommendation that the situation be studied in more detail before hooking up the computers as planned. On June 3, Margaret sent the memo to her superior, Project Director Inder A. Singh, outlining the danger as she saw it. She felt that he would agree with her suggestion that a study be initiated to analyze the situation more carefully and formulate recommendations. She was shocked when she received a very direct "No" to her request. Singh told her not to pursue the matter any further and ordered the computers to be hooked up as originally planned.

Margaret was faced with a difficult choice. She could go along with her orders, continue in her current position, and advance in the organization as a capable, loyal employee. On the other hand, she felt an obligation, reflected in her professional code of ethics, not to consent tacitly to a questionable action that could lead to harm to patients and even loss of life. She hoped for a while that she could reach a resolution of this difficulty by requesting a transfer to another project with the commissioner of health. At least she would not then be directly involved with the questionable practices. After a few days on this new project, however, Margaret was still having qualms about what would occur if the new system were hooked up as planned. She finally decided that she should speak up and do whatever was possible to prevent this system from going into effect. She sent another detailed memorandum to Singh reiterating her concerns. She was met with an even stronger statement that she should drop the matter at once.

Against Singh's orders, Margaret decided on June 17 to send a detailed report to the next level of management in her organization: the members of the MHPC. She hoped that someone with influence on that committee would speak up on a matter about which she herself was powerless to do anything more.

She sent her memo the following day. On June 24, Margaret received an official letter of termination of her employment. Singh stated his official reasons clearly enough:

> The termination . . . was effected because (1) your distribution of the memorandum to members of the MHPC committee was in direct violation of a policy established by me, and (2) it was against expressly given orders that all communications sent to the members must be approved by the Project Director.

The MCC of the IEEE conducted an investigation of Margaret's case. They found that she had adhered to the IEEE code of ethics and was qualified to discern the potential for degradation of the intensive care monitoring system. They also found that her discharge constituted seriously improper treatment of a professional. Her actions on behalf of the patients were regarded as a considerable personal sacrifice, in keeping with the highest tradition of professionalism in engineering.

The MCC contacted the health commissioner, the director and chairman of the MHPC project, and the deputy mayor for health services. The deputy mayor and director replied by stating that the issue raised by Clinton was receiving careful attention by the city. Neither, however, could offer the MCC any specific studies or actions that had actually been taken.

The MCC concluded that Clinton was acting properly under the code of ethics. They contended (1) that she was qualified to discern the potential degradation of the police emergency system by virtue of her professional training; (2) that she attempted to inform her project director; and (3) that her attempt to inform the Criminal Justice Steering Committee represented an attempt in good faith to protect community interests. It was the committee's opinion that her termination resulted from her efforts to avoid compromising her professional responsibilities and to abide by the IEEE's code of ethics.

The Outcome

Was Margaret Clinton a success? It is difficult to answer this question conclusively. According to Richard Vincentti, the deputy mayor of the MHPC, the ACPAS system was never installed. Whether or not this resulted directly from Clinton's actions is difficult to say.

From a personal point of view, she waged and lost a tough battle. On the positive side she gained the respect and credibility of her peers — other members of the IEEE. The MCC published an article that concluded:

> We believe the circumstances of the situation described herein indicate the present need of employers to develop a means whereby professional employees can raise and be afforded review of their judgments, responsibly formulated, so as to avoid their summary discharge for violation of "policy," when the result of such policy serves to prevent the dissemination and reasonable consideration of professional opinions related to the successful functioning of systems or equipment involving safety and welfare considerations, directly or indirectly, affecting the public interest of a community of citizens to be served by such systems or equipment.

She was also given an award for Outstanding Service in the Public Interest by the CSIT-IEEE. "Winning it," according to Margaret, meant saving lives, which in turn meant not risking an overload of the computer system. As she put it:

> If indeed we were correct that it would be overloaded (which we never said it would, we just said you must look at it, you don't

just throw stuff in there), then we would have saved lives and . . . won. So I feel that we had a chance of winning. At the very least, we did win a delay anyway.

On the other hand, she was tormented throughout the episode. Psychologically, she was set back, her self-image was threatened and for some time she feared that she might suffer a nervous breakdown.

From an objective, as opposed to a personal perspective, can she be judged a success? To judge the success of a whistleblower, one must ask each of the following questions:

1. Was the wrongdoing stopped?
2. Were the whistleblower's concerns shown to be unfounded?
3. Was there a change in policy?
4. Was the organization prosecuted or convicted?
5. Were people able to avoid becoming victims?

In answer to the first question, wrongdoing was stopped. Even if the system had not become overloaded, it would have been wrong to hook it up because of the potential dangers. In answer to the second, Margaret's concerns were not unfounded. In fact, the evidence indicates that they were soundly based. Third, Richard Vincentti and Stephen Dworkin both stated that the ACPAS system was initially going to be installed, but according to Vincentti it never was. Fourth, while the organization was not prosecuted or convicted, it was reprimanded by the IEEE. Finally and most important, nobody was hurt. Perhaps patients are a little safe today for Clinton's actions.

Margaret Clinton took on a very difficult task: a very difficult organization. The MHPC is a complex and far-flung organization for even a professional and a professional association to tackle. To understand her dilemma is to understand the MHPC — its history and structure.

THE MUNICIPAL HEALTH PLANNING COUNCIL

The MHPC, established by the office of the mayor in 1967, is responsible for the planning, coordination, and implementation of hospitals and clinics across the city. Members of the council, the health services coordinator, and the director are appointed by the mayor. The full council has 35 members, but only 23 members constitute the Executive Committee and have voting privileges.

Included among the members of the council are the health inspectors in the five boroughs; the heads of hospitals and clinics, several city councilmen, and judges; and citizens who represent neighborhood associations. The full council meets on an average of once a year. According to Stephen Dworkin, general council for the MHPC, a meeting of the full council is usually held whenever a new administrator from the federal Department of Health (DOH) comes to town to address them. The Executive Committee, on the other hand, meets about five times a year. Their meetings are open to all members and also to the public at large.

At these meetings the board votes on grant proposals prepared by both public and private agencies to determine which applications to fund with DOH and city money. The DOH gave money to the state of Illinois through the Division of Health Services, which in turn allotted funds to the city of Chicago. It was the responsibility of the MHPC to disseminate the funds in an equitable fashion among the city's health agencies and on-line organizations. Vincentti, health services coordinator (formerly called deputy mayor for health services), had an informal policy that attempted to divert 25% of the available funds to community clinics and preventive programs. Often this was not possible, owing to the cross section of line agencies represented on the council. The various heads of hospitals carried a lot of weight on the council, and their requests usually received the necessary funding. However, staff could affect policy in that they more or less chose which of the grant proposals to present to the council. Grant proposals would come in and, depending on the substantive area, were assigned to the respective program personnel. The program people would work with applicants and help prepare a modified proposal, if needed. The proposal would then be passed along to the next levels of review — the health services coordinator and finally to the Executive Committee.

The MHPC is a small city agency. It has a professional staff of between 40 and 50 employees at present. According to Dworkin, it began with around 30 employees, growing at one time to between 70 and 100 employees. This growth was due in part to an attempt to get funding for things they could not handle internally. For example, the Budget and Planning Task Force grant was secured to coordinate all the various information systems throughout the health services system. Three other grants also increased personnel. The Performance Evaluation Unit is the largest, with a staff of six evaluators. The Health Services Information Systems grant and the Comprehensive Planning Unit both have three or four professionals plus a secretary.

The executive staff of the MHPC was composed of the health services coordinator, Vincentti; the director of the MHPC, Sontag; the deputy director; the executive assistant to the director; and the general counsel, Dworkin.

The health services coordinator is the mayor's adviser on health services matters. He is responsible for reviewing budget requests from health services agencies, increasing cooperative efforts among them and taking on special assignments from the mayor. He reports directly to the mayor.

The director and deputy director are responsible for the daily operations of the agency. Dworkin, while serving as general counsel/chief of operations, oversaw the fiscal operations and the audit functions and was responsible for providing the Executive Committee with information. He had a small legal staff that mainly did research on DOH guidelines. Dworkin reported directly to Vincentti.

The agency was divided into six so-called planning units, which in essence were grant processing units. The divisions were Hospitals, Clinics, and Health Inspections units. These reported to the project coordinator.

Grant proposals were assigned to the division having programmatic responsibility. To facilitate the delivery of services, additional units were set up. The Fiscal Unit performed a desk audit function on the grants already under way in the city of Chicago, particularly the private agency grants. Governmental agency grants were audited by the Division of Health Services. The Grant Review Unit was similar to an Office of Inspector General. It was composed of one officer on loan from Chicago's Health Department and two other staff people. The Personnel/Administrative Unit consisted of one office manager and a number of secretaries. Prior to February 1981, personnel and payroll were handled by the Chicago City Civil Service Office. As the agency became more sophisticated, the Central Control Unit was formed to track the funding information on the grants, for example, how much money was being spent. Neither Dworkin nor Vincentti mentioned the Monitoring Unit's responsibilities. These units reported to the general counsel.

According to Vincentti, policy evolved out of DOH and Division of Health Services rules and regulations and was set by him in consultation with the director and his executive assistant. Larger decisions were made by the Executive Council.

Professional disagreements were handled routinely through the chain of command. If personnel problems reached Vincentti, he was guided by the director's recommendation. The disagreement between Margaret Clinton and Inder Singh, her superior, involved a difference in professional judgment. Clinton, according to Vincentti, was not saying anything that had not already been discussed. It was understood that they might need an additional computer. Singh understood that it might indeed slow response time, but he was willing to wait and see, as there were ways that computer programmers could recognize this. Vincentti elected to go with Singh — the more experienced technician.

Stephen Dworkin, although he prefaced his remarks by stating that he had no firsthand knowledge of the incident, believed that she "went public" to the MHPC before there had been any opportunity for the MHPC Project Committee to discuss it. In other words, she did not voice it adequately within the committee meetings, which were open to anyone. All the health services heads — the commissioners and various heads of hospitals — made up the MHPC committee. They met once a month to establish priorities. Singh, the MHPC project director, reported to Herbert Sullivan, who was district attorney for Manhattan and chairman of the MHPC project. He also reported to Vincentti through the director, Sontag.

PROFESSIONALISM, POLITICS, AND PROTEST

Margaret Clinton's case is a classic example of conflicting loyalties. On the one hand, she has obligations to her employer to be loyal and conscientious; on the other hand, she has obligations as a professional to protect the life and safety of clients and the public at large.

Specifically, in her case she was one of two computer experts who shared general responsibility for the operation of an IBM 360. As an employee of the MHPC she was responsible to Singh who, like her, was also a computer specialist.

The installation of a ACPAS system to help hospital administrators manage their billings caused a crisis that led her to write a series of memos and eventually to blow the whistle by going outside the MHPC to a professional association, the IEEE.

The basic issue in her case is: How much input should a professional have into the policy-making process? Should her professional judgment carry the day? Clearly, she thought yes, and Singh thought no.

As a professional she believed that she held a public trust to use her skills and knowledge for the public as well as the private good. As a computer specialist she felt bound by its code of ethics, which required her to protest when she believed that the public safety was threatened. Since the ACPAS system would possibly impair the operation of the PAMOS, her protest seemed to her morally justified.

Singh, on the other hand, saw the issue in managerial terms. Decisions have to be made. Professionals can have input into these decisions, but they cannot preempt them. Eventually, a policy decision must be made by those with the responsibility for making decisions. As he subsequently asserted, to give professionals the kind of autonomy Clinton demanded would place professional societies in the position of running the organization — instead of management.

What is the central issue? Are we concerned with a technical decision or a managerial decision? Should policy be set by politics, politicians, and the political process or by skilled, informed professionals? Two issues need to be separated: Who should decide and how should decisions be made?

Since Clinton worked within a public agency, one could argue, public officials should make the final decisions — through the political process. The decision to be made is: Should the ACPAS system be hooked into the PAMOS system? Given that to do so would degrade the effectiveness of the PAMOS system already in place, the question then becomes: How much degradation is permissible? This question resembles a similar, oft-debated one: What constitutes an acceptable level of risk?

One of Clinton's tasks is to determine how much risk or degradation is likely. She can also offer professional advice in suggesting ways this risk might be avoided — perhaps by hooking the ACPAS system into the backup computer instead of the main computer. If there is some way to avoid the risk, she as a professional should try to discover it and report it to those with the authority to implement it.

Clinton believed that an alternative existed and hence that the risk was unnecessary. No reason was given for the rejection of her alternative. If we assume that there was a good reason — for example, that it was important to keep the backup system intact — then the question returns: How much influence should she exercise on policy decisions?

Singh criticized her for failing to exercise an option that was available to her: to attend the meeting of the MHPC committee and voice her concerns there. These meetings were open to the public generally, and she could have criticized what had happened there. Her reasons for not doing so reveal more of her personality than morality: she was a shy person, not politically astute and probably awkward in a public forum. Hence she is not going to attack the head of the MHPC committee in public and risk humiliation, embarrassment, or retaliation.

Given that this option was available to her, what right of protest does she have if she fails to exercise it? Some critics of civil disobedience have insisted that breaking the rules of the legal game in protest is unwarranted in a democratic society because one has alternative legal means to change laws one finds morally objectionable. One could argue, by analogy, that her protest outside the organization violated the rules of corporate conduct — given that she had other means to express her disapproval. Given that her reasons for rejecting this alternative were personal rather than professional, how far are her superiors obliged morally to go to accommodate her predilections?

Perhaps, as Singh suggested, no general answer to this question is possible. Each organization, each professional association, and finally each individual must decide for themselves.

GUIDE QUESTIONS

1. Do you think the decision to add the ACPAS system onto the PAMOS system was primarily a technical one for computer scientists or a policy decision for management?
2. How much input should a professional have into policy decisions? For example, do you think that a computer scientist should have a veto power in policy matters?
3. How could you do a cost-benefit calculation on the installation of the new ACPAS system onto the old PAMOS system?
4. "It was really up to nurse Sarah Livemore to have blown the whistle — it was the patients who stood to be harmed and as nurse she was responsible for their welfare." State whether you agree or disagree and why.
5. If you were in Singh's position and under pressure from the accounting department, what would you do?
6. Suppose the IEEE found Margaret's fears unfounded, would Singh's firing her then be justified?
7. Do you think the courts could or should effectively protect Margaret Clinton?
8. Do you think it would have been better for Margaret to have gone to the media? Would she have gotten more effective action? Would it have been disloyal?
9. Do professional societies, such as the IEEE, offer adequate protection for professionals? Is there anything more they could do?
10. At what point should a professional association be contacted and when, if ever, is it justified in intervening?
11. Would she have been justified in going directly to the IEEE when she first learned of the impending installation, or is she morally obliged first to make some effort to resolve matters internally?
12. Should a professional society play only a factfinding role or can it also serve effectively as a mediator or disciplinary agent?

13. What would you have done in Margaret Clinton's position? In Sarah Livemore's? In Inder Singh's?
14. Do you think it is wrong to dismiss a professional employee for adhering to his or her code of professional conduct?

SEVEN
LIFE, SAFETY,
AND THE
INSPECTOR GENERAL

WORLD'S FAIR CONSTRUCTION BEGINS

Dallas, Texas — Ground breaking ceremonies were held today for the new U.S. Pavilion Complex. The facility, with an estimated cost of $25.5 million will house the U.S. space exhibit at the World's Fair to be held in August 1981. The building contains an indoor track, an olympic size swimming pool, and a convention hall with a seating capacity of 8,500. The City of Dallas will be responsible for its maintenance after the Fair.

The U.S. Department of Budget's Federal Financing Administration (FFA) is providing approximately $45 million to the World's Fair Organizing Committee's $61 million construction budget. FFA recently opened a local office downtown on Center Street. Project engineers will be monitoring the construction of ten other separate facilities.

On hand for the ceremonies this morning were. . .*

*Front Page of the *Dallas Times*, February 13, 1978.

FFA ENGINEER SAYS WORLD FAIR PROJECTS UNSAFE

Dallas, Texas — Two project engineers on the construction sites charged today that building projects for the World's Fair were shot full of unsafe and dangerous practices.

In an unusual press conference held this morning, Nick Boylan and Richard Cook, project engineers for the Federal Financing Administration, said, based on preliminary investigations, there is a "significant" possibility that the public would be endangered by going into the US Pavilion Complex.

> Contacted late this morning, the World's Fair Organizing Committee press office had no comment. An official statement is expected tomorrow.*

*Front page of the *Dallas Times*, May 5, 1980.

NUTS AND BOLTS

Nick Boylan was an obviously talented and energetic young engineer. Before assuming the position of Federal Financing Administration project engineer in March 1978, he had distinguished himself with several awards and had written a book on structural steel that had become the "bible" of the industry. Yet the issues he was to face in this job were not those of strict professional competence and judgment but of personalities, politics and finance.

He had overall responsibility for the safety of the buildings, a job for which, in principle, he was well suited. Nick took his responsibilities very seriously and insisted that the letter of the regulations be observed. His enthusiasm was not well received.

That enthusiasm led him to uncover questionable construction practices. Joints that should have been safety secured were left loose. Trusses that should have been joined were left dangling. He brought these problems to his supervisor's attention as he discovered them, and tried to persuade the contractor to correct them. His concerns were typically brought up in an informal manner with Andrew Hartman, the federal engineering director.

One early incident involved a missing brace in the U.S. Pavilion, and Nick was asked by Andrew to write up a chronology of this problem. According to Nick:

> I prepared the chronology and Andrew said we might as well send a copy to Washington to Jack Reid, Project Management Director. When Reid read that we were getting into the nuts and bolts, not just the general principles, he got very angry. He called to say, "You guys aren't supposed to be getting involved in these kinds of details unless they involve health and safety."

Andrew thought to himself, "They certainly do involve life and safety." But he and Reid held back their anger. Nick and his superior proceeded to follow up the matter in a conscientious way.

Many other construction practices became a concern to Nick: lack of structural safety in the new U.S. Pavilion, carbon monoxide poisoning, disregard for the federal and state laws and requirements for access to handicapped persons, lack of inspection at construction sites, and numerous other matters concerning life and safety.

Nick went to a variety of state and federal agencies with his concerns. He called the local Occupational Safety and Health Administration office about construction-related air pollution in the area. He notified the Texas Department of Health about the carbon monoxide problem, and telephoned the Department of Budget's Office of Auditing and Finance about his concerns regarding the construction. At the same time, in an attempt to remedy these problems informally, he regularly met with the contractors and members of the World's Fair Organizing Committee.

The Committee, composed of 50 members from the metropolitan area of Dallas, oversaw the construction and was responsible for making sure that its principal contractor, the Harland Construction Company, followed all federal, state, and local laws and regulations. Weekly meetings were held to discuss the problems and their respective solutions. Usually in attendance were representatives of the FFA, Harland, and members of the Committee.

Andrew brought problematic concerns before the committee:

> The questions that I would normally raise would require some answers which weren't available at the time, but by the next week's meeting, the matters would be addressed. We continually forced a planning process and an implementation process.

Nick continued to encounter opposition. It was a frustrating situation for him as he attempted to secure the necessary adjustments to protect the public's health and safety. He received lip service from most of the agencies contacted. In February 1979, almost a year since his appointment, the resistance hardened — he was banned from the construction sites! How was he supposed to do his job?

> There is no question in my mind that it was retaliation. I had my responsibilities reduced in half because I simply was not allowed to go on any construction sites.

The ban, according to Andrew, was a result of pressure on FFA headquarters applied by the contractors and the Committee.

> His approach to dealing with matters was very curt and not necessarily diplomatic. In the process of dealing with issues,

whether major or minor, he was taken as offensive for two reasons. First, he called attention to matters that should have been corrected, but weren't and therefore caused personal embarrassment. Second, in attending the Committee meetings, he seemed to be continually pointing the finger. If you looked at who requested the ban, it was the guys he would be embarrassing, and he would be showing them up in a bad light. I received a couple of letters and several telephone calls to keep him the hell out.

FFA officials in Washington received similar calls. Gary Fisher, the newly appointed project management director who ordered the ban, said, "Notwithstanding the possible validity of Nick's complaints, I am opposed to the manner in which he communicated them at the job site."

Although confined to office duties, mainly processing change orders, Nick did not desist in his efforts. With Andrew's encouragement he surreptitiously visited the construction sites. But after several months, he realized that this approach would not work. Memo after memo outlining the structural design and faulty workmanship problems were being ignored by members of the Committee and FFA headquarters. There were too many problems, on too large a scale, to be addressed in this manner.

His problems came to a head during one of these early morning inspections. The swimming pool was housed in Building One of the U.S. Pavilion Complex and had a reinforced glass roof. The structure, like a table turned upside down, was supported by 20 steel pillars secured at the top of the roof. The pillars were supposed to be held in place by bolts that were reinforced with welds at 20 places on each beam. The bolts were not there. Instead their place was taken by additional welds that Nick worried were not sufficient to ensure the safety of those who would use the building. The building was dangerous, and the faults needed to be corrected before it was opened to the public.

Nick reported the problem to his superior. They inspected the site together and agreed that the welds were insufficient to support the roof. When they contacted the project manager for Harland, he explained that the welding was a necessary substitute for the bolts because of a faulty design for which he was not responsible. Nick was not satisfied. Whoever was at fault, something needed to be done.

THE INSPECTOR GENERAL INTERVENES

The FFA, which administered the grant to the Committee, had a twofold responsibility: first, to make sure that the job was done the most economical way possible; and second, to meet all of the construction specifications and requirements. The Committee was likewise accountable for both fiscal and safety matters. Andrew comments:

> I don't think anyone in government had ever had a position of this type, and I don't think anyone could have envisioned the kinds of activity one individual would be involved in (financial, engineering, environment, construction, and public relations). Prior to this time, government had never been involved in the World's Fair. One of the difficult things was the fact that we funded it at 100% financing, and that's contrary to the way we operate as an agency.

The field office in Dallas, although relatively autonomous, reported directly to the FFA headquarters, and had administrative linkages with the regional office in Denver. According to Andrew, this ambiguity created problems.

> Operationally, there was no one in charge, no one to tell me what to do or when to do something, and that situation existed for most of the tenure of the project.

This lack of organizational structure, with no clearly defined chain of command, inevitably had important impact on the subsequent flow of events. Decision making occurred on a day-to-day basis and involved quite a bit of individual discretion. The lack of any firm policies or procedures to guide individuals when major problems arose was a glaring error from a number of people's viewpoints. Andrew, for instance, mentions:

> I think the lack of support was probably one of the major failings, the lack of personnel support that is. When I say personnel support, I mean legal assistance that I needed very badly and that contributed to a lot of the confusion.

Almost a year and a half into the project, Andrew and his staff received the needed personnel support. In lieu of legal assistance, auditors were assigned to the Dallas office in late 1979. Nick's memoranda and his weekly telephone calls to the Office of Auditing and Finance, in conjunction with the recently passed Inspector General Act, were the motivating factors.

Pursuant to the legislation, the newly organized Office of Inspector General (OIG) within the Department of Budget was assigned the functions formerly vested in the Departmental Office of Auditing and Finance and the Investigations and Inspection staff of the FFA. They had the responsibility for investigating alleged criminal violations and program abuses. The OIG was divided into two primary operating organizational units: the Office of Audits and the Office of Investigations and Inspections.

In early 1980 the OIG issued an audit report that listed 15 separate deficiencies and defects in the construction of the U.S. Pavilion Complex. The report, based on information Nick provided, recommended that an independent engineering firm be commissioned to certify the facility's structural integrity. An additional seven audit reports were compiled during the next several months, not all of which dealt with safety issues. Auditors examined such matters as post-Fair use of the facilities, financial costs, the possibility of mismanagement and fraud, and lack of contractually required inspections. According to Brooks Arnold, the chief auditor, Nick was invaluable.

> Nick provided us with a monthly update on what he perceived as problem areas. And we were doing a lot of correspondence back and forth on what we were doing to attempt to resolve these problem areas.

Since the appointment of Alice Michaels, the first Department of Budget inspector general, the OIG became more involved. Nick recalls:

> As construction continued and I discovered more design and construction errors, I felt we needed an investigation. First, I tried to convince my superiors in FFA that they should look into all of this and have it corrected. When they swept it under the carpet and refused to do it, then I went outside of FFA, but still within the Department of Budget, to the new Inspector General.

Nick hoped that she would give him the support he needed to accomplish his objectives and to cut off all interference. It was his responsibility to see that the buildings were constructed in accordance with the plans and specifications and the conditions of the grant, but the OIG did not move as swiftly as Nick wanted. The Committee was procrastinating in signing a contract with Wilding Contractors, the firm chosen to do the structural evaluation. Arnold remembers the reasons for the delay:

> Whenever you enter into a contract, especially when you're not sure exactly what you want done, there's always problems and negotiations, and it always takes longer. It's very difficult to get

the contract awarded and implemented in a short space of time, no matter what the procurement is. So there was a delay between the time we actually made the initial recommendation and the time Wilding was brought in to do the study on the Complex.

All reports issued by the OIG are advisory, but according to Michaels, "We have enough clout in the Department of Budget, where if the recommendations aren't acted upon, we can go directly to the Secretary of Budget." The recommendation for an investigation, however, was acted upon. Wilding began its evaluation in mid-March.

The OIG was also instrumental in having the restrictions lifted so that Nick could once again monitor the construction sites. In several memos to Victor Kaiser, deputy assistant secretary for budget, she recommended that Nick's full responsibilities be reinstated. By the end of March, the ban was rescinded.

Upon returning to the job sites on a daily basis, Nick encountered bigger and more pressing problems. He discovered a lot of financial abuse, fire-safety violations, and additional serious construction flaws. Time was running out: the World's Fair was only five months away. Believing that nothing would come out of the investigation, Nick seriously thought about going to the press with his allegations. At one point prior to the appointment of Michaels, John Callahan, the acting inspector general, had told him:

> Sometimes the only way you can get things done in government
> is to go through the press.

What Callahan was implying concerned the trade-offs for himself. As Nick stated:

> If I went to the press, he had everything to gain but nothing to
> lose. If he had started the investigation, he had everything to
> lose but nothing to gain.

Nick lacked confidence in the OIG. It was a new system and he believed that:

> Inspectors general are political appointees and are no different
> than any other appointed official or Congressman. They are
> always going to be weighing their theoretical duties and respon-
> sibilities against the practical aspects of surviving in their posi-
> tions.

"ROUND 14": THE FIGHT CONTINUES

About this time, Richard Cook, another conscientious and dedicated FFA engineer, was fired. Richard had been confronting similar violations and shoddy construction practices on the Visitors' Lodging project. Both he and Nick believed that his discharge was retaliatory. He, like Nick, had been pressuring contractors to conform to construction and design specifications. The Visitors' Lodging project, according to Richard, did not meet the Texas Building Code for fire safety. His concerns included the inadequacy of fire alarm systems, and the number of exits.

Both engineers realized the need for immediate action. Their first order of business, after they had made the decision to contact the media, was to arrange for a press conference. Nick contacted the *Dallas Times'* city editor, who in turn invited representatives from the media to attend. The editor, in exchange for keeping the nature of the press conference confidential, requested that it be timed so that he could get his article out before anyone else.

The following week, the press conference was held as scheduled. Before discussing their specific allegations, Nick articulated his reason for the meeting:

> We hope you, the media, will be able to accomplish what we've been unable to do; that is, to insure that the World's Fair will be structurally safe, environmentally sound, accessible to the handicapped, and cost-efficient.

The press conference received front-page coverage all across the country. The initial reaction from FFA officials was restrained, consisting of memos requesting him to clear matters with the department's press office in Washington before talking to the press. One such memo from Vic Kaiser read:

> As of this date, the final report of the commissioned analysis has not been received. While awaiting these results, any day-to-day contacts between you and the grantee or its agents would be detrimental to our overall working relationship. . . . Your action in conducting a press conference at this time, and under these circumstances, reflects poor judgment and is not the proper manner in which to address such issues.

The relationship between Nick and Andrew began to change dramatically. Andrew summarized his reaction to the press conference:

I was absolutely, positively teed off because it was a complete surprise, and I felt that we could have handled matters differently. They (the committee) held me totally responsible. . . . I was the bad guy.

From being close friends and associates on and off the job, their relationship continued to deteriorate to the point where they were outright enemies. According to Nick:

Once you have blown the whistle, maybe not immediately, but very soon thereafter, it's equivalent to getting the bubonic plague. People just want to steer clear of you totally. This was Andrew's reaction as well as everybody else's. They feel that if they are friendly to me, then by association they may be laid off, fired or whatever.

One minor incident involved the relocation of Nick's desk. Andrew sent him a memorandum informing him that his desk was to be moved to the conference room. Each of the five staff members concurred that they suffered "an inability to concentrate on their normal work functions" because of his "continued relaying of information contained in business discussions to the press and other outside sources."

A more serious indication of the tension between the two men transpired a few weeks later. Nick accused Andrew of assault. His statement to the personnel management specialist assigned to investigate the allegation read:

Andrew Hartman entered my office and asked me whether I expressed concern to Alice Michaels, the Inspector General, about his involvement with the World's Fair facilities after they had been turned over by the Federal Government to local interests. After telling Andrew Hartman that I did, he made various threats of physical violence and grabbed me by the vest. While attempting to defend myself, I was hit on the forehead; had my chair overturned, causing me to bump my head; and had my vest torn. I then called Alice Michaels, and then the local police.

On the other hand, Andrew stated:

I entered Nick Boylan's office and asked if he had made any allegations regarding my forming a private corporation in collusion with the World's Fair Organizing Committee to manage the facilities after they had been turned over to local interests. Mr. Boylan responded that he had done so. . . . I suggested that he cease to arbitrarily remove and copy correspondence from the files for distribution to the press and others. I further suggested that he not assume that I wouldn't take whatever action is necessary to prevent this type of action on his part. I then proceeded to leave his office without ever physically touching Mr. Boylan.

The OIG suggested that an internal hearing, chaired by an impartial party, he convened. However, the personnel management specialist concluded:

The information obtained by the certifications and police report is inconclusive in that it does not verify the full account proclaimed by either party. Neither individual has been able to provide evidence or witnesses to substantiate their claim that. . . . *We do not have meaningful information that allows us to make a conclusive decision.*

Based on the report, no disciplinary action was taken against Andrew, and although contrary to the OIG's recommendation, no hearing was held.

A SECOND LOOK

Wilding Contractors scheduled a press conference in early June at which time their findings would be released to the public. Nick, however, was banned from attending. Once again, he sought help from Alice Michaels. Eventually, she helped work out a compromise between Kaiser and Nick. Kaiser granted Nick permission to attend on the stipulation that if a question were addressed to him during the conference, he would answer that he had no comments.

At the press conference the U.S. Pavilion Complex was given a clean bill of health by Wilding Contractors. A spokesman said that the questions raised by Nick were dismissed upon examination because corrections had been made, that conditions said to be deficient were structurally adequate, and that the concern was based on misunderstanding or misinformation. Only minor flaws were reported to have been found. The corrective work involved checking and improving welded connections in horizontal roof trusses where faults had been found.

Nick was still not satisfied. When he visited the site to check on the remedial welding, he discovered further problems. Additionally, in going over the lengthy Wilding report, Nick realized that the

X-rays used by Wilding to verify the connective welds were not representative. He brought this immediately to Michaels' attention. The possibility of a roof collapse under stress was still too great. The OIG had to do something and do it quickly, for the World's Fair was only months away.

Michaels, upon learning of this disparity, contacted Kaiser and other FFA officials. Her task was clear: to convince them that Wilding should do a more thorough on-site inspection. The Committee, however, hesitated. At this stage of the project, money was tight and they had had enough of Nick Boylan. But owing to pressure from the OIG, the Committee extended Wilding's contract to cover inspection of the roof's welds. As a result of this second evaluation, workers had to reweld some of the connections, and added steel plates to each of the 20 steel members connecting the roof to the building. With only weeks to spare, the U.S. Pavilion Complex was declared safe once and for all. Both Wilding and Nick agreed that all major flaws had been corrected.

The following week Nick received a "thank you" from FFA officials — it was a reduction-in-force notice that he would be separated from employment effective the following month. Nick was hired on a term appointment, which ranges from one year to four years, and his original date of separation was still months away. Because he believed that the notice was retaliatory, he sought protection from the OIG.

Alice Michaels responded by contacting Vic Kaiser. In one letter she wrote:

> The termination of Mr. Boylan, if effectuated before the end of his term, raises the question as to whether a reprisal is being taken against him for making a complaint or disclosing information to my office. . . . In order to ascertain whether the proposed termination is, in fact, retaliatory, we will require access to your records relating to Mr. Boylan.

At the end of the month, Nick received a letter from the personnel office that read:

> Based on a reassessment of the workload, Deputy Assistant Secretary Kaiser has determined that your continued employment is warranted. . . . This rescinds the reduction-in-force notification.

With the assistance of Michaels, Nick continued to fulfill his responsibilities as project engineer until the expiration of his term appointment.

EPILOGUE

BOSTON ARENA LOSES ROOF IN STORM

Boston, Mass. — The roof of Jackson Arena collapsed last night in heavy rain and high winds. The arena was empty, though 15,000 people had attended a rock concert there the night before.

This morning, the arena's exterior was largely intact, but the interior was a mass of rubble, with the bright Boston sun shining through a hole almost 200 feet square onto the twisted remains of ceiling trusses and yellow insulation panels.

Peter Donahue, project engineer for Harland Construction Company who directed the firm's construction of the arena, said "It could have been an uplift caused by the wind that caused the roof to collapse, or it could have been simply a case of weight causing a cave-in."

The arena met all of Boston's building code regulations about wind resistance and weight, and was checked out by two independent engineering firms before being constructed.

Boston officials refused today to estimate the amount of time . . .*

*Front page of the *New York Times*, May 16, 1983

Given that there seems to have been no reform in the industry, what could be done by engineers like Nick Boylan or the inspector general? Where should we go from here?

GUIDE QUESTIONS

1. Do you think Nick Boylan was justified in holding his unauthorized press conference?
2. Do you think he exhausted all internal avenues before going to the media?
3. What would you have done with Boylan if you were his superior?
4. What role, if any, do you think the media played in the resolution of Boylan's concerns?
5. Do you think Boylan received adequate protection from the Office of Inspector General?
6. Do you think a public agency can fairly and effectively investigate itself through an Office of Inspector General?
7. Since the Dallas field office had ambiguous reporting relationships to both Denver and Washington, how might future field offices be set up to deal with a whistleblower's allegations effectively?

SUGGESTED READINGS

Baran, Andrew. "Federal Employment — The Civil Service Reform Act of 1978 — Removing Incompetents and Protecting 'Whistleblowers.'" *Wayne Law Review* 26 (1979): 97–118.

Coven, Mark. "The First Amendment Rights of Policymaking Public Employees." *Harvard Civil Rights-Civil Liberties Law Review* 12 (1977): 381–406.

Government Accountability Project. "Analysis of the Inspector General Act of 1978." Washington, D.C.: The Institute of Policy Studies, 1979.

Lindauer, Mitchell J. "Government Employee Disclosures of Agency Wrongdoing: Protecting the Right to Blow the Whistle." *University of Chicago Law Review* 42 53061.

Nickel, Henry. "The First Amendment and Public Employees — An Emerging Constitutional Right to Be a Policeman?" *George Washington Law Review* 37 (December 1968): 409–424.

Public Law 95-452. "Inspector General Act 1978."

Sanders, Wayne. "Constitutional Protection For Whistle Blowers: Has the First Amendment Called in Sick?" Paper presented at the Eleventh Annual Convention of the Popular Culture Association combined with the Third Annual Convention of the American Culture Association, Cincinnati, Ohio, March 29, 1981.

U.S. Congress, Senate. Committee on Government Affairs. *Establishment of Offices of Inspector and Auditor General in Certain Executive Departments and Agencies*, 95th Cong., 2d sess., 1978.

Vaughan, Robert G. "Public Employees and the Right to Disobey." *Hastings Law Journal* 29 (November 1977): 261–295.

APPENDIX: THE INSPECTORS GENERAL

On October 12, 1978 President Jimmy Carter signed a bill that reorganized the executive branch of the government and increased its economy and efficiency by establishing Offices of Inspector General within 12 federal departments and agencies. Public Law 95-452, or the Inspector General Act of 1978 as it is commonly called, consolidated existing auditing and investigative resources to combat more effectively fraud, abuse, waste, and mismanagement in the programs and operations of those departments and agencies.

Recent evidence, brought to light by the press and government officials, pointed out that fraud, waste, and abuse in federally funded programs had reached epidemic proportions.

Other proponents of the act cited deficiencies in current federal efforts to combat fraud and waste, particularly lack of resources and deficiencies in organizational structure.

Most agencies simply did not have the resources to prevent, much less detect, abuses. For example, the Department of Transportation had only four inspectors to detect fraud in a $6 billion highway program. The Veterans Administration had one auditor for every $238 million provided by Congress.

Previous federal audit and investigative efforts failed, according to a General Accounting Office report, because auditors and investigators reported to, and were under the supervision of, the very officials whose programs they were supposedly auditing and investigating. The chief of the Community Services Administration's Inspection Division testified that he had been denied permission to investigate allegations of wrongdoing in several cases. In one such case a later investigation resulted in 22 indictments.

The inspector general concept is based on the premise that for the audit and investigate capacity to be effective authority must be vested in an individual reporting to, and under the supervision of, only the head of the agency. The act not only mandates this but further states that the head of the agency may not prohibit, prevent, or limit the Inspector General from undertaking and completing any audits and investigations which the Inpector General deems necessary.

This legislation creates positions of inspector general in the Departments of Agriculture, Commerce, Housing and Urban Development, the Interior, and Labor and Transportation and within the Community Services Administration, the National Aeronautics and Space Administration, the Veterans Administration, the General Services Administration, the Environmental Protection Agency, and the Small Business Administration. Their duties and responsibilities include: (1) providing policy direction for the auditing and investigating activities of the agency; (2) reviewing existing and proposed legislation and regulations relating to programs and operations of the agency and to Congress concerning the enforceability of such legislation and regulation; (3) supervising other activities for the purpose of promoting economy, efficiency, and effectiveness in the administration of such programs or preventing or detecting fraud and abuse in such programs; (4) coordinating relationships between the agency and other federal agencies, state and local governmental agencies, and non-government entities; and (5) keeping the head of the agency and Congress fully and currently informed concerning fraud and other serious problems in the operation of programs.

The inspector general system is best described as the consolidation of auditing and investigative responsibilities under a single high-level official. It is designed to address the major problems confronting current federal efforts to prevent or detect fraud and abuse.

First, the legislation provides a single focal point in each agency for the effort to deal with fraud in federal expenditures and programs. Heretofore, the linkage between investigating and auditing was ineffective owing to decentralization of audit units. Some decentralized units were responsible for certain elements of a wide-ranging programmatic fraud but were unable to pursue them to their conclusion. Additionally, a single office strengthens cooperation between the agency and the Department of Justice in investigating and prosecuting fraud cases. The Justice Department reports that those agencies that have been the most effective co-partners have been those with viable Offices of Inspector General. [The Departments of Agriculture (1962) and Housing and Urban Development (1972) created the Offices of Inspector General administratively. In 1976, Congress created the first statutory inspector general at the Department of Health, Education, and Welfare.]

Second, because the inspector general is a presidential appointee, confirmed by the Senate, it is clear that Congress takes the problem and responsibilities seriously, thereby upgrading the auditing and investigative functions in the executive agencies.

Third, the act gives the inspectors general no conflicting policy responsibilities that could divert their attention; their sole responsibility is to coordinate auditing and investigating efforts.

Fourth, the inspectors general have the requisite independence to do an effective job. They are under the general authority of the head of the agency, and not under the supervision of any other official in the agency.

Fifth, because the inspectors general can provide and set forth publicly "best estimates" of current fraud, waste, and abuse in agency programs and operations, Congress and the public derive benefit. Once a problem is identified, management can begin corrective steps. Stricter legislation can be adopted.

Inspectors general prepare semi-annual reports in order to disseminate their findings. The reports, initially forwarded to the agency head and later to Congress, are available to the public. They summarize a description of significant problems, abuses and deficiencies relating to the administration of agency programs; recommendations for corrective action; and matters referred to prosecutive authorities and the prosecutions and convictions that have resulted.

In addition to investigating mismanagement, waste, or fraud, the inspector general may receive and investigate complaints or information from an employee of the agency concerning abuse of authority or a substantial and specific danger to the public health and safety. Moreover, the Civil Service Reform Act of 1978 requires that if a complaint is brought to the attention of the special counsel, he or she should refer the complaint to the agency head for investigation. Consequently, the inspector general may receive not only complaints from employees but also those that come indirectly from the special counsel via the agency head. Both the Inspector General Act and the Civil Service Reform Act protect the complaining employee by stipulating that the inspector general or special counsel may not disclose the complainant's identity unless they determine that such disclosure is unavoidable during the course of the investigation. Furthermore, no employee is to suffer retaliation as a result of making a complaint or disclosing information to these government officials.

EIGHT
THE COURTS:
THE PHYSICIAN VERSUS
THE DRUG COMPANY

DEPOSITION OF DR. JOYCE JARDIN

DATE: July 10, 1979

Q: Please state your full name, occupation and age.

A: Dr. Joyce Jardin. I am a physician. I am 57 years old.

Q: By whom were you employed in 1976, and what were your responsibilities?

A: I was a research physician employed by Fisher Pharmaceutical Corporation. Basically, I tested drugs and investigated and monitored drug studies.

Q: What was your salary at that time?

A: $48,500 a year.

Q: With whom did you interact in the normal course of your work?

A: Well, I was under Dr. Eric Von Eichvorn, the Research Director, and Dr. Michael Singer, the Research Associate Director. I was also in touch with the U.S. Food and Drug Administration.

Q: Did you ever disagree with your superior, Dr. Von Eichvorn?

A: Yes. We had a conflict of viewpoints concerning the use of a drug on humans which I was responsible for, that finally led to my resignation.

Q: Could you tell me more specifically how the conflict led to your resignation?

A: The drug they (management) were asking me to test on humans contained a high level of saccharin. It was an anti-diarrheal liquid formulated for infants, children, old people, and other patients who could not take solid medication. The high level of saccharin was condemned by the team of people I worked with — until finally we were ordered to proceed with all haste to write the protocols, study the design, and prepare to market this drug.

In the meantime the team I worked with, fearing the potential carcinogenic characteristics of saccharin, began pursuing an alternative formulation which would either eliminate the saccharin or at least substantially reduce its level in the drug. We knew that an alternative formula could be developed within three months.

The conflict between Dr. Von Eichvorn and me involved not only medical judgment but also the question of propriety. It was my duty as the only physician on the team to ask doctors to prescribe this test drug to infants and children to study its effects. Knowing an alternative could be reached in three months without the high saccharin, I could not with a clear conscience ask that any person be needlessly exposed to a potential carcinogen.

Q: Now, how did this lead to your resignation?

A: Well, these pressures mounted over several months, until the end of March 1977. Then, the edict came down that I and the rest of my team must use the liquid formulation. From that time on there was strong opposition to me.

Q: What do you mean by "strong opposition"?

A: The team accepted management's directives. But I felt that since I was the only physician on the team I, alone, was responsible for exercising sound medical judgment. I was the one who must distribute this to the investigators to use. It was nice that the team wanted to get the project done but then the responsibility of marketing this controversial formulation rested with the only expert — me.

Then my superior, Dr. Von Eichvorn, called me into his office and told me he was taking me off the team, I said "Do what you must — you're the boss." He told me I lacked judgment and was irresponsible. He said that both he and the Research Associate Director considered me unpromotable.

Q: Doctor, in your complaint in this matter it is indicated that when you became a physician you took a Hippocratic Oath which obliged you to uphold certain ethical standards which you would have violated had you continued on the *filiomide* project. Is that so? Did, you, in fact, take such an oath?

A: Yes.

Q: Did anyone ask you to violate that oath?

A: Yes.

Q: Would you please elaborate?

A: If I had accepted the high saccharin formulation, as Dr. Von Eichvorn directed, I would have violated the oath. One section requires physicians never to knowingly cause harm to another. I have with me the relevant section which I would like to read.

I swear . . . that I will fulfill according to my ability and judgment this oath and this convenant: . . . I will apply dietetic measure for the benefit of the sick, according to my ability and judgment; I will keep them from harm and injustice. I will neither give a deadly drug to anybody if asked for it, nor will I make a suggestion to this effect.[1]

THE CONFRONTATION

Dr. Jardin came to Fisher Pharmaceutical Corporation in the spring of 1971 as senior research physician. Fisher was a member of the Bailey Hygiene, Inc., family — 11 companies that manufactured medical and hygiene products. In addition to hygienic supplies, their scientific laboratory developed anti-bacterial agents and commercial drugs.

During her first years at Fisher, things went well for Dr. Jardin. The company was enjoying steady growth and was emphasizing the development of new drugs. Dr. Jardin, having earned a solid reputation in development and testing, was promoted to one of the top level research positions in the company.

Her colleagues admired and respected her professional abilities and personal fortitude. She was known among them for her scientific excellence and "level-headedness." When practices did not meet her rigorous standards she pursued the issue and somtimes stood up to management if necessary.

One such instance, strikingly similar to the present situation, arose when she was employed as a medical officer for the Food and Drug Administration (FDA). She resigned when her group did not issue prompt warnings about the possible harmful side effects of birth control pills. Current research on "the pill's" side effects has borne out her suspicions.

Prior to the company's directive to move forward with the marketing of the EMOLIO drops (a cough suppressant), Dr. Jardin had enjoyed a good working relationship with both the team and her superior, Dr. Von Eichvorn: "I thought we worked well together even though I was more qualified than Dr. Von Eichvorn and the other members of my team, that is, to practice medicine."

Initially, the team fully supported Dr. Jardin, believing that the formula was too dangerous and that a saccharin substitute needed to be developed to counteract the formula's bitterness. The team expressed their concern and made recommendations to the company. Dr. Jardin and the others expected routine approval.

Early in April, one of the senior members submitted a memorandum in which he summarized the team's objections:

> In view of the possible carcinogenic effects that the artificial sweetener, saccharin, may have on consumers we, the project team, cannot recommend marketing the present formula. There is substantial evidence available to indicate that saccharin causes cancerous tumors after a seventeen year latent period.
>
> We recommend developing an alternative, safer formula which can be taste tested for acceptability by the marketing department.

Management was resolutely determined to manufacture the drug in spite of their knowledge that an alternative would be available within three months. The following minutes of a March meeting stated the company's position:

SUBJECT: EMOLIO PEDIATRA MEETING
March 28, 1975

A meeting was held to discuss the future direction of the developmental effort for EMOLIO Pediatra.

As a result of meetings with Dr. Herzman of Eidelmann Medical Company, it was determined that Eidelmann Company will market EMOLIO Pediatra Drops (2mg./ml.).

As the conflict unfolded, the rest of the team acceded to the increasing pressure. As Dr. Jardin stated:

The team was very much together until management said "run with this and do it." But then they all acquiesced — unable to stick with a decision that was scientifically based.

By mid-April, several members of the team decided to accept management's orders rather than fight a losing battle. At a project meeting on April 18 the majority voted to "proceed with due haste" on the clinical testing of filiomide. Three days later Dr. Jardin reaffirmed her position to the team and asked for their support.

Dr. Jardin believed the marketing department had a strong interest in EMOLIO. As far as she was concerned, Fisher Pharmaceutical's primary objective was "to make money — this is the heart of corporations in the drug business. Their motivation to do good for humanity is only secondary."

She attempted to resolve the matter internally by talking to Dr. Von Eichvorn:

If you would let me present this honestly to the FDA, the way the situation is, and they would say "don't worry about it," I would go ahead. Or if you would let me go to three unbiased persons, consultants, outside of the company, and ask them if they felt that this was a proper course, I would go ahead.

Dr. Von Eichvorn did not agree. Rather, he criticized her "unprofessional and irresponsible" behavior.

After her resignation, Dr. Jardin consulted with an attorney, decided that she had good grounds for legal action and initiated a suit against the company. She wanted an impartial arbiter to resolve the issue as fairly as possible: she would not only accuse

Fisher Pharmaceutical of wrongdoing, but she would also allow the company to counter her argument and defend itself. Once the matter had gone through the court, she was willing to abide by its decision — pro or con.

If nothing more, the issue would at least become a matter of official record. It would be heard openly — by the public, the medical community, Fisher Pharmaceutical, the FDA, and lawyers.

Although she might have gone directly to the media with her story, she preferred the court. Her view might appear lopsided if she relied on the press alone. Even though she did not report to the media directly, she benefited by its coverage of the court.

THE COURT

Court Chronology

In May 1977 Dr. Jardin filed a complaint alleging *constructive dismissal*. This legal term means the employee was effectively fired even though he or she may have quit. Several months later Fisher Pharmaceutical filed a motion for summary judgment, a legal strategy that requests the court to rule in favor of the drafter — in this case Fisher, arguing that:

1. resignation barred a suit for wrongful discharge;
2. even assuming Dr. Jardin's employment could be construed as a discharge, she was still an employee at will;
3. even if construed as a discharge, no important public policy was violated by terminating her employment;
4. there was no material issue of fact;
5. a jury should not decide a medically debatable issue.

In January 1978 an order granting Fisher Pharmaceutical's motion for summary judgment was signed. Dr. Jardin appealed in March 1979 to the superior court, law division. Her brief argued that the summary judgment must be denied because:

1. material facts were involved;
2. a plenary hearing would determine Dr. Jardin's state of mind (she alleged that she was under duress when she resigned);
3. important public policy issues were involved that reached beyond the case;
4. Dr. Jardin was constructively discharged;
5. Dr. Jardin's employment contract was violated;

6. refusal to obey an unreasonable or unlawful order did not justify discharge;
7. Dr. Jardin's property right, to work at her chosen trade, was violated; and
8. Dr. Jardin's discharge contravened public policy.

The case was remanded for trial.

The Fact Finder's Statement

I wish to thank both counsel for their detailed and exhaustive presentation in their briefs and in their oral arguments. Indeed, this is a critical matter.

According to the documents filed, Mrs. Jardin is a physician who worked for the defendant, Fisher Pharmaceutical Corporation, between 1971 and 1975. She began as Senior Research Physician, and in 1973 assumed the role of Director of Medical Research. While in the latter capacity she was assigned to a project team of individuals working on the drug known as *filiomide* (same formula as EMOLIO).

In early May 1975, Dr. Jardin indicated to Dr. Von Eichvorn, her superior, that she disagreed with the decision made by the project team to test the formulation of the drug because of what she considered to be an excessively high amount of saccharin in the syrup.

There has recently been much discussion concerning the potential carcinogenic properties of saccharin in medical journals, magazines, and newpapers.

On May 9, 1975, she was formally notified that she would be relieved of her responsibilities for the *filiomide* pediatric project.

On May 14, 1975, she met with Dr. Von Eichvorn who, it is alleged, criticized several aspects of her job performance. At that meeting Dr. Von Eichvorn asked Dr. Jardin to consider another project in medical research on which she would consider working (Dr. Jardin describes this offer as a demotion — lessened responsibilities).

On June 16, 1975, Dr. Von Eichvorn again met with Dr. Jardin and reiterated the criticism made at the first meeting. He stated that Dr. Jardin would be taken off the project and again asked which projects in medical research she should pursue.

On June 17, 1975, the day following the second meeting, Dr. Jardin submitted a written resignation to Dr. Von Eichvorn, which, in its pertinent parts, provided as follows:

> Upon learning in our meeting of June 16, 1975 that you believe I have not acted as a director; have diplayed inadequacies as to my

competence, responsibility, productivity, and ability to relate to marketing personnel; that you, and reportedly Dr. Michael Singer, Research Associate Director of Development, and Mr. William Brown, President of Fisher Pharmaceutical, consider me to be unpromotable; and that I am now or soon will be demoted; I find it impossible to continue my employment with Fisher Pharmaceutical.

This resignation was accepted by Dr. Von Eichvorn according to his memo dated June 18, 1975.

On May 7, 1977 (almost two years later), Dr. Jardin filed suit against Fisher to recover damages resulting from the termination of her employment. Her written statement setting out grievances, which was served on the defendant and filed with the court, contains five counts:

1. It is alleged that because of Fisher Pharmaceutical's actions, Dr. Jardin sustained damage to her professional reputation, interruption of her career, forfeiture of interesting and remunerative employment, monetary loss, deprivation of retirement benefits, loss of four years' seniority, physical and mental distress, and pain and suffering.
2. It is alleged that the company breached its contract of employment with the plaintiff in refusing to permit her to use her expertise, skills and best medical judgment.
3. It is alleged that the defendant, by its actions, isolated the plaintiff's property right in the form of her expertise and skill in the field of pharmaceutical research.
4. It is alleged that the defendant interfered with her employment contract and relationships.
5. It is alleged that the defendant violated and interfered with her right to object to the appropriate regulatory bodies presumably with regard to the safety of *filiomide*, the drug with which the plaintiff had previously been working.

Professional Employees at Will

Dr. Jardin's vulnerability to discharge for actions she felt were required of her by professional standards exemplifies a pervasive legal restraint on professional behavior: the ability of employers to discharge arbitrarily a professional employee without incurring liability. Ethical behavior may conflict with the need of management to pursue profit. Lawrence Blades has pointed out several situations in which this conflict may arise.

Consider, for example, the plight of an engineer who is told that he or she will lose his or her job unless the individual falsifies data or conclusions, or unless he or she approves a product that does not conform to specifications or meet minimum standards. Consider also the dilemma of a corporate attorney who is told, say in the context of an impending tax audit or antitrust investigation, to draft backdated corporate records concerning events that never took place or is told to falsify other documents so that adverse legal consequences may be avoided by the corporation. Or consider the predicament of an accountant who is told to falsify his or her employer's profit-and-loss statement in order to enable the employer to obtain credit.[2] The resolution of such conflicts between the employer and the ethical employee frequently takes the form of discharge, demotion, or other retaliatory actions such as reprimands, criticism, loss of support, and pressure to resign.[3] While employers and employees should be encouraged to behave ethically, the law arguably inhibits such principled behavior. The employment-at-will or fire-at-will doctrine has for over a century given employers absolute power to discharge an employee "for good cause, for no cause, or even for cause morally wrong, without being thereby guility of legal wrong."[4]

The Majority Opinion

Fisher Pharmaceutical responded by petitioning the Supreme Court for certification. In July 1980 the highest state court, in a final binding decision, reversed the lower court's decision and reinstated summary judgment in favor of Fisher Pharmaceutical. The court reasoned that Dr. Jardin had erred in:

1. Not relying on a specific provision of the code of ethics;
2. Failing to recognize the substantive countervailing (public) interest in the development of drugs, subject to the approval of a responsible management agency like the FDA, and;
3. Failing to demonstrate that her allegations of potential public harm were predicated on something more substantial than a mere difference of opinion.

The North Carolina Supreme Court denied Dr. Jardin's action to recover damages from her employer, but the majority did hold that an at-will employee has a cause of action for wrongful discharge if it is contrary to a clear mandate of public policy. Plaintiffs in such cases would be required to cite a specific, clear expression of public policy in order to invoke the exception. Although the court allowed this exception to the doctrine, it denied its application for Dr. Jardin, reasoning that "her continued participation in the development of *filiomide* would not have violated any clear mandate of public policy."

The majority decision emphasized the lack of an immediate threat to public health at the time Dr. Jardin refused to work on the "controversial" drug. It also found that Dr. Jardin had no basis because she failed to cite a specific provision in the American Medical Association's code of ethics.

According to the court, the only tenable cause of action available to Dr. Jardin was that the filing of an application with the FDA was unethical, but Dr. Jardin failed to include this allegation in her complaint. It concluded that the "general language" of the Hippocratic oath "does not prohibit, specifically, research that does not involve tests on humans and cannot lead to such tests withiout governmental approval."

The majority feared that "chaos would result if a single research doctor was allowed to determine, according to his or her individual conscience, whether a project should continue." It reasoned that one doctor's personal decision not to proceed should not halt an entire, perhaps worthwhile, medical project.

The majority opinion is binding and final, but the dissenting opinion presents some of the ethical issues that bear on this case. The dissenting justice agreed with the majority that the employment-at-will doctrine should be modified to include a public policy exception but disagreed because he thought that the new ruling should have been extended to Dr. Jardin.

The Dissenting Opinion

I agree with the majority's ruling that a professional employee may not be discharged for refusing to violate a clearly recognized legal or ethical obligation imposed on members of her profession. However, the majority's application of this principle defies logical explanation and disregards the established judicial doctrine on the propriety of the judgment. The majority further errs by assuming that the absence of a written agreement signifies beyond dispute that the plaintiff's employment was strictly at the will of the drug manufacturer. I therefore respectfully dissent.

The court pronounces this rule for the first time today. One would think that it would therefore grant the plaintiff the opportunity to seek relief within the confines of this newly announced cause of action. I fail to see how the majority reaches this conclusion.

There are a number of detailed, recognized codes of medical ethics that proscribe participation in clinical experimentation when a doctor perceives an unreasonable threat to human health. Any one of these codes could provide the "clear mandate of public policy" that the majority requires.

The opportunity to prove a discharge in violation of public policy is not based solely on recognized codes of professional ethics. There is also a legislative prohibition on conduct by physicians that endangers life or health. To regulate the professional behavior of doctors, the legislature has empowered the State Board of Medical Examiners to grant, suspend, or revoke licenses to practice medicine within the state. The statute enumerating the Board's powers provides in part:

> The Board may refuse to grant or may suspend or revoke a license . . . to practice medicine . . . upon proof of gross malpractice or gross neglect in the practice of medicine which has endangered the health or life of any person . . .

If the plaintiff could prove that the defendant discharged her for refusing to engage in "gross malpractice", the defendant would be liable for violating a "clear mandate of public policy."

The majority denies the plaintiff the opportunity to demonstrate that her discharge was a response to her refusal to violate statutory policy as well as several codes of medical ethics. I fail to understand why. Nothing is more unfair than stating a novel principle of law for the first time but denying the plaintiff who sought relief under some new standard an opportunity to conform her proof to the specific requirements actually adopted. Yet it appears the majority has done precisely that.

Three other points by the majority require discussion. The first is the majority's characterization of the plaintiff's ethical position. They believe that Dr. Jardin had the power to determine whether the defendant's proposed development program would continue at all. This is not the case. The plaintiff claims only her right to professional autonomy. She contends that she may not be discharged for expressing her view that the clinical program is unethical or for refusing to continue her participation in the project. Moreover, it is undisputed that the defendant was able to continue the program by reassigning personnel. Thus, the majority's view that granting doctors a right to be free from abusive discharges could obstruct desired drug development is ill-conceived.

The second point concerns the role of governmental approval of the proposed experimental program. In apparent ignorance of the past failures of official regulation to safeguard against pharmaceutical horrors, the majority implies that the necessity for administrative approval for human testing eliminates the need for active ethical professionals within the drug industry. But we do not know whether the United States Food and Drug Administration would have been aware of the safer alternative formulation. Autonomous professionals within the drug industry are a necessity.

The final point to which I must respond is the majority's observation that the plaintiff expressed her opposition prematurely — before the FDA had approved clinical experimentation. Essentially, the majority holds that a professional employee may not refuse to engage in illegal or unethical conduct until her actual participation and the resulting harm is imminent. This principle grants little protection to the ethical autonomy of professionals that the majority proclaims. Would the majority have Dr. Jardin wait until the first infant was placed before her, ready to receive the first dose of a drug containing 44 times the concentration of saccharin permitted in twelve ounces of soda? A professional's opposition to unethical conduct should not be considered untimely when its unethical nature is apparent.

The plaintiff has been denied the benefit of the rule which she has sought to vindicate her professional conscience. Since I would permit her that benefit, I respectfully dissent.

POSTSCRIPT

Dr. Jardin began to reconstruct her life. After applying to several drug companies as a research scientist and receiving no offers of employment, she realized that she must move to private practice in order to resume her career.

In spite of her request for denied damages, a monetary defeat, she felt that her intentions were accomplished:

> Right from the beginning I understood that Fisher was a giant, and I'm very little; and I didn't expect anything. I hoped to make a point — which I did. I thought the chances of any kind of reasonable settlement from Fisher were just about nil — and they were. But I think they remembered me, and they remember the issue. Now it has been debated publicly and it's done a little bit of good, so I feel I've fulfilled my obligation. Many people were informed, especially doctors, who might otherwise have remained uninformed and unconcerned . . . I sleep well at night.

Fisher never did proceed with the testing and marketing of loperamide.

GUIDE QUESTIONS

1. Do you agree with the majority or the dissenting opinion?
2. Should Dr. Jardin have resigned?
3. If you were the president of Fisher, how would you have handled Dr. Jardin?
4. What motives, other than profit, does management have? Are there any other management issues (e.g., public image or time invested in training Dr. Jardin)?
5. Is the drug industry more vulnerable to professional dissent than other industries?
6. How might Fisher's management be restructured to keep a similar incident from occurring?
7. If you were a member of the team, what would you have done?
8. Do you think the fear of the majority that one doctor's decision not to participate might halt the entire project is well founded?
9. How can professional codes restrict the employment-at-will doctrine?
10. Should professional codes be built into the laws?
11. How satisfactory was the court in addressing Dr. Jardin's professional, as opposed to personal, concerns?
12. Did Dr. Jardin pursue the best strategy under the circumstances? And did she pursue it effectively?

NOTES

1. Ludwig Edelstein, "The Hippocratic Oath," in *Ancient Medicine*, ed. Oswei Temkin and C. Lillian Temkin (Baltimore, Md.: Johns Hopkins University Press, 1967).
2. Lawrence Blades. "Employment at Will versus Individual Freedom: On Limiting the Abusive Exercise of Employer Power," *Columbia Law Review* 67 (1967): 1404.
3. Kelly lost his staff and funding: Jardin was called "irresponsible and unpromotable" by her superior; Boylan was ostracized.
4. *Payne v. Western and A. R. R.*, 81 Tenn. 507, 319–520 (1884); and *Hutton v. Watters*, 132 Tenn. 527, 179 S.W. 134 (1915).
5. The Declaration of Helsinki of the World Medical Association, adopted in 1962, established guidelines for conducting medical experiments on humans. The American Medical Association adopted ethical guidelines for clinical investigations. See Judicial Council, AMA, Opinions and Reports of the Judicial Council. The Nuremberg Code states principles included in the Nuremberg Military Tribunal's decision of *U.S. v. Karl Brandt*.

SUGGESTED READINGS

Blades, Lawrence E. "Employment at Will v. Individual Freedom: On Limiting the Abusive Exercise of Employer Power." *Columbia Law Review* 67 (1967): 1404–1435.

Blumberg, Phillip I. "Corporate Responsibility and the Employee's Duty of Loyalty and Obedience: A Preliminary Inquiry." *Oklahoma Law Review* 24 (August 1971): 279–318.

Christiansen, Jon P. "A Remedy for the Discharge of Professional Employees Who Refuse to Perform Unethical or Illegal Acts: A Proposal in Aid of Professional Ethics." *Vanderbilt Law Review* 28 (1975): 805–841.

Committee on Labor and Employment Law, The Association of the Bar of the City of New York. "At-Will Employment and the Problem of Unjust Dismissal." *Record* 36 (April 1981): 170–216.

Conway, John H. "Protecting the Private Sector At Will Employee Who 'Blows the Whistle': A Cause of Action Based upon Determinants of Public Policy." *Wisconsin Law Review* (1977): 777–812.

Feliu, Alfred G. "Loyalty, the Employment Relationship and the Law." Paper presented at the Conference on Conflicting Loyalties in the Workplace at Bentley College, Waltham, Mass., April 2, 1982. Mimeographed.

Malin, Martin. "Legal Protection for Whistleblowers." Paper presented at the Second Annual Conference on Ethics in Engineering, Chicago, Ill., March 5–6, 1982. Published in *Beyond Whistleblowing*, ed. Vivian Weil (Chicago: Illinois Institute of Technology, 1984).

Peck, Cornelius J. "Unjust Discharges from Employment: A Necessary Change in the Law." *Ohio State Law Journal* 40 (1979): 1–4.

Protecting At-Will Employees against Wrongful Discharge: The Duty to Terminate Only in Good Faith." *Harvard Law Review* 93 (1980): 1816–1844.

Rice, Thomas. "Judicial Limitations of the Employment at Will Doctrine." *St. John's Law Review* 54 (Spring 1980): 552–579.

Schneier, Mark. "Public Policy Limitations on the Retaliatory Discharge of At-Will Employees in the Private Sector." *University of California (Davis) Law Review* 14 (1981): 811–837.

Solomon, Lewis D., and Terry D. Garcia. "Protecting the Corporate Whistleblower under Federal Anti-Retaliation Statutes." *Journal of Corporation Law* (Winter 1980): 275–297.

Summers, Clyde W. "Protecting *All* Employees against Unjust Dismissal." *Harvard Business Review*, January/February 1980, pp. 132–139.

Walters, Kenneth D. "Your Employees' Right to Blow the Whistle." *Harvard Business Review*, July/August 1975, p. 29.

Youngblood, Stuart A., and Gary Tidwell. "Termination At-Will: Some Changes in the Wind." *Personnel*, May/June 1981, pp. 22–33.

APPENDIX I: THE HIPPOCRATIC OATH

I swear by Apollo, Physician, and Asclepius and Hygieia and Panaceia and all the gods and goddesses, making them my witnesses, that I will fulfill according to by ability and judgments this oath and this covenant:

To hold him who has taught me this art as equal to my parents and to live my life in partnership with him, and if he is in need of money to give him a share of mine, and to regard his offspring as equal to my brothers in male lineage and to teach them this art — if they desire to learn it — without fee and covenant; to give a share of precepts and oral instruction and all the other learning to my sons and to the sons of him who has instructed me and to pupils who have signed the covenant and have taken an oath according to the medical law, but to no one else.

I will apply dietetic measures for the benefit of the sick according to my ability and judgment; I will keep them from harm and injustice.

I will neither give a deadly drug to anybody if asked for it, nor will I make a suggestion to this effect. Similarly I will not give to a woman an abortive remedy. In purity and holiness I will guard my life and my art.

I will not use the knife, not even on sufferers from stone, but will withdraw in favor of such men as are engaged in this work.

Whatever houses I may visit, I will come for the benefit of the sick, remaining free of all intentional injustice, of all mischief and in particular of sexual relations with both female and male persons, be they free or slaves.

What I may see or hear in the course of the treatment or even outside of the treatment in regard to the life of men, which on no account one must spread abroad, I will keep to myself holding such things shameful to be spoken about.

If I fulfill this oath and do not violate it, may it be granted to me to enjoy life and art, being honored with fame among all men for all time to come; if I transgress it and swear falsely, may the opposite of all this be my lot.

APPENDIX II: THE EMPLOYMENT-AT-WILL DOCTRINE

The employment-at-will doctrine is based on the implicit contract between an employee (who was hired for an indeterminate period of time) and his or her employer: either party may terminate the contract at any time for any reason.

Thus, an employer may dismiss an employee for any reason without being guilty of any wrongdoing. Conversely, an employee may quit under the same conditions.

This was not the rule in early English law.[1] At that time the law presumed that employment was intended for a fixed duration — usually one year.[2]

The late nineteenth and early twentieth centuries gave birth to the employment-at-will doctrine. The national mood of laissez-faire capitalism and its corollary belief in the freedom of contract dominated the economy. The new rule was well suited to the "rustic simplicity of the days when the farmer or small entrepreneur . . . was the epitome of American individualism."[3] The court advocated what it considered to be equal rights of employees and employers.

> The right of a person to sell his labor upon such terms as he deems proper is . . . the same as the right of the purchaser of labor to prescribe the conditions upon which he will accept such labor from the person. . . . [T]he employer and employee have equality of right, and any legislation that disturbs that equality is an interference with the liberty of contract.

The employment relationship is subject to regulation by federal, state, and local governments. Employers are prohibited from discharging or disciplining employees for numerous reasons — participation in collective bargaining; unionizing; discrimination against race, color, religion, sex, or national origin; political activities; jury duty; or refusal to take a lie detector test. Employees are protected in every state from employment believed to be dangerous because of physical conditions. A few states have even passed "whistle blower bills", which forbid reprisals by employers against employees who report violations of the law to authorities.

APPENDIX NOTES

1. Feinman, "The Development of the Employment-at-Will Rule," *American Journal of Legal History* 20 (1976), 118.
2. Id. at 120 (citing Blackstone, *Commentaries* 1: 425).
3. Blades, "Employment at Will," sup. n. 2, at 1416.

NINE
THE CONGRESS AND NUCLEAR DISSENT

ALERTING CONGRESS

Jeff Thomas boarded the plane to Washington. Over the past few months he had made this trip several times from his Michigan home. This time, however, he was not interested in casual conversation with his fellow passengers: his mind was on more important matters. In less than six hours he would be sitting before a U.S. Senate committee. The committee was holding hearings on energy-related topics, including the safety of nuclear power plants. They would provide a perfect opportunity for him to express his views — to make his concerns known to a national forum.

He had serious doubts about the integrity of the nuclear industry's design and management philosophy, and it was crucial that they be heard. Several of his colleagues were aware of the many problems associated with nuclear power but, for one reason or another, chose to remain silent. Those who viewed themselves as narrow specialists with fragmented roles in the system simply preferred not to rock the boat. Others were optimistic and thought that eventually all the problems would be resolved. After all, the nuclear industry was still in its infancy.

At times like this Jeff wished he were more confident in his public-speaking ability. He had never had trouble getting his point across on a one-to-one basis, but in front of a large audience his thoughts and ideas did not flow as freely. Maybe Bruce Arnold realized this when he suggested that he insert Jeff's paper, critical of the industry, into the *Congressional Record*. Bruce was an eloquent speaker and as a result was often called upon to testify on behalf of environmental groups. Today he would be representing the Friends of the Earth and wanted the paper as support for their position. Trained in law and conversant on nuclear power issues, he had the expertise and confidence to respond to questions posed by legislators. Jeff lacked that spontaneity.

The fact that Jeff would not be testifying directly before the committee did not bother him. As long as his concerns were heard and his recommendations acted upon, the means of dissemination did not matter. He hoped that his proposals would be given consideration and that Congress would force the industry to implement the reforms he suggested. He wanted to convince the public, through Congress, that the industry was so badly managed that it had no business criticizing foreign nuclear plants. The evidence that nuclear power plant systems were sold before they were properly designed would motivate a congressional analysis of the present state of the nuclear industry. He was sure of it.

With the landing of the plane in Washington, Jeff's thoughts temporarily focused on the more immediate task of securing a taxi. On the way to the Capitol he wondered if Bruce was equally nervous and what consequences would follow regarding his own career with Atomic Engineering — a nuclear engineering consulting group. Norm Lawrence, the president of Atomic Engineering, would be displeased to say the least, but Jeff defended his decision to go public by virtue of his right to speak as a private citizen and his serious concerns for the public welfare. No mention of Atomic Engineering was made in his paper and, in fact, it was the industry as a whole, not his employer, with whom he found fault. It was true, though, that through his employment he had obtained the evidence (documents, reports, and memoranda) of some careless practices by clients that had led him to doubt the industry. His duty to protect the public interest, as embodied in the engineering code of ethics, outweighed his obligation as an employee to his organization. The public's safety was at issue.

Bruce was waiting for him in the Rotunda. Everything was running like clockwork — that was a good omen. They even had time for a leisurely lunch before the three o'clock hearing. Several people recognized Bruce and came over to exchange greetings. He definitely possessed the requisite political skills to propose needed legislative remedies. Jeff began to relax. Although he was well informed, Jeff's credentials were weak. Industry leaders might not consider a line engineer qualified to address such global issues as centralization of quality assurance, project management, and standardization of design. Congressional members, however, might view his experience with diverse nuclear power management as a reliable indicator of present management practices. Jeff's paper, the culmination of a lot of hard work, weekends spent in libraries, a voluminous amount of reading, and the analyses of data, reports, and memorandums, was made a matter of public record that afternoon. Upon seeing the glaring television lights and crowded room filled with reporters, senators and an endless parade of witnesses, he was quite relieved to have relinquished the task to Bruce. He was not disappointed: Bruce did an excellent job of presenting his views. The senators seemed to be interested and receptive to the ideas presented. At the end of his paper, he had formulated a list of recommendations that he encouraged Congress to implement: tighten up quality assurance (QA) practices by creating an Office of Quality Assurance; insist on third-party inspection of components of nuclear power plants and plant systems; and compare the contract management evident in the National Aeronautics and Space Administration (NASA) to the contract management typical of the nuclear industry. Only time would tell whether he had convinced them to act.

Both men believed that they had chosen the most appropriate forum. As a government body, Congress wielded the power necessary to bring about reform. The problems confronting the nuclear power industry were of national importance and should be resolved by representatives empowered to make decisions on a national level. Other options were less attractive.

The courts, a strategy available for redressing an alleged personal wrongdoing, did not constitute a viable alternative. His complaint, that the industry's managment philosophy lagged behind technological development, did not indicate a violation of some law or regulation. Rather, it was prompted by the poor management practices of industry leaders.

Jeff believed that the media, another external option for dissidents, was extremely sensitive to pressure from the nuclear industry. Reporters hesitated to investigate controversial and complex matters, especially such generic concerns as those voiced in his paper. Without a detailed series of articles devoted to explaining the terminology and related nuclear issues, the average reader would be unimpressed with the newsworthiness of his complaint. Hence, a newspaper would fail to recognize the benefit of publishing the story. This option was in Jeff's mind, however, as he left the hearing. He had not completely rejected that strategy. If Congress failed to implement the needed reforms, he would take his case directly to the people through the media. Muckraking often worked, although he hesitated to use such tactics.

Community or environmental groups were already playing a role, albeit a small one. A representative of the Friends of the Earth had already been scheduled to appear before the committee when Jeff decided to release the paper. It was only coincidental that both shared analogous goals. His concerns were not amenable to marches down Pennsylvania Avenue or rallies in front of nuclear power plants: the issues were too complex. The utility of this option would cease with the disclosure of his paper. Similarly, professional engineering groups, not organized for lobbying and lacking the necessary clout, could not serve as a vehicle for change.

One final option he considered was the Atomic Energy Commission (AEC). In 1954 the AEC began its dual role of promoting and regulating commercial nuclear power. From its inception, the AEC vigorously promoted commercial exploitation of the "peaceful atom." Given the overriding commitment of the federal government to rapid nuclear power expansion, AEC's role in the effort was largely pro forma: the political decision had already been made to proceed with a large-scale nuclear program and to accept the risks involved. But the AEC adopted a relaxed and permissive regulatory program. A small number of its staff engineers and consultants reviewed the applications for nuclear plant licenses, but the commission sometimes ignored safety issues they raised. Like industry leaders, the AEC was convinced that technological solutions to these problems could be deferred and eventually remedied. The conflict of interest inherent in the AEC's dual responsibility to promote and regulate told Jeff that this agency would be of little assistance in resolving the matters addressed in his paper.

The ride back to his hotel had taken less time than he thought. It was still early, but his mind and body were exhausted. The strain of the day was beginning to take its toll. In Michigan Norm Lawrence would be returning from lunch. As Jeff relaxed on the bed, he could visualize him sitting behind his huge antique desk in his leather chair, far removed from the events of this afternoon. His thoughts turned to his organization. Was the industry to blame for the faults his paper listed, his employer, the government, or who? What role did his company play: perpetrator, collaborator, witness, or innocent victim? Jeff wondered what Norm's goals were when he established Atomic Engineering.

SERVING THE CUSTOMER

Norm founded Atomic Engineering in the early 1970s to aid in developing nuclear energy as a safe and efficient power source. It provided the industry with engineering and technical services in all phases of the power-generating process — from conceptual design of power plants to the operation and eventual decommissioning of these facilities. By the end of their first full year of operation, Atomic Engineering had 12 employees and 15 clients and had generated revenues of about half a million dollars. Increasing in both personnel and profits over the next few years, Atomic Engineering had grown to over 200 employees by 1975. From 80 to 90 percent of these persons were practicing engineers at the line level, with only a handful of managers.

Perhaps this growth had been too rapid. Engineers were shifted into managerial positions with little or no training. In an attempt to remedy this imbalance, Atomic Engineering provided its employees with sorely needed managerial training and offered tuition refunds for employees attending college. The opportunities were adequate, but the training was not specifically focused on industry-wide problems. Instead, training and educational programs tended to be limited to developing cooperative relationships with employees and clients and learning to manage the workload effectively. As a result, their engineers and managers were not prepared to confront complex policy questions posed by nuclear dissidents.

In only a few years Jeff's organization had developed strong technical and marketing capabilities, notably in quality assurance services, start-up and testing assistance, and sophisticated analytical capabilities. Quality assurance programs and records management systems, in which Jeff played a role, provided many clients with administrative quality control over equipment, purchasing, inspections, and testing.

In 1973 Jeff was hired as a quality assurance specialist by Robert Neubauer, a senior vice-president and partner. He developed computerized systems, but several of his recommendations were rejected. For example, he designed a pilot management information system that would consider management problems at a deeper level. However, clients were not interested, and Atomic Engineering made no attempt to convince clients of its worthiness. It occurred to him that the industry did not want management advice, only technical assistance.

While serving as a consultant within a host organization, Jeff usually reported to the plant superintendent. This, however, was only a courtesy. For in reality his immediate superior was one of the several project engineers within Atomic Engineering who often had to divide their time among several projects. Immediately above the project engineer in the chain of command was the manager of the project. In all there were about six such positions. Neubauer, the vice-president, represented the next highest level. The final authority rested with Norm Lawrence, president of the company.

Since Atomic Engineering was a small organization in the early 1970s, many administrative functions were under the control of one person, rather than distinct offices. For example, one accountant handled the fiscal affairs for the organization. Lawrence's secretary was responsible for personnel matters. Jeff never understood the arrangement. Was Atomic Engineering relegating personnel matters to the back burner by allowing a secretary to handle grievances? Or did it mean that employee complaints received management's immediate attention because the president's secretary was invested with these responsibilities?

Policies and priorities were set by the two partners: Lawrence and Neubauer. The main priority, Jeff was told many times, was to serve the customer! Serving the customer had various connotations, however. Most of their consulting engineers interpreted it to mean doing the best possible engineering job while maintaining the status quo. Accordingly, their responsibilities did not encompass anything more than merely providing technical assistance for the resolution of immediate problems. Because their continued employment was dependent upon the industry's demand for their expert services, they lacked the incentive to address long-range problem areas.

To Jeff, serving the customer meant safeguarding the public. That required questioning the integrity of the nuclear power systems, challenging the lack of industry standards, and calling attention to chronic problems. In the end, both the customer and the public would be served.

He found fault with his organization for its lack of leadership. Atomic Engineering, as a reputable consulting firm, should be playing a more active role. Jeff believed that there were two ways his organization could accomplish this.

First, it could provide the leadership for developing industry-wide standards. Their clients ran the gamut of differences in nuclear power plant management, where effective solutions could originate and be tested. By standardizing systems across plants, Atomic Engineering would be taking a step in the right direction.

Second, his organization could openly address the problems as they surfaced. If corporate officials reported these problems, as opposed to a line engineer, the impact on the industry would be much greater. By ignoring the problems, however, his organization was an accomplice in the continued whitewash of the nuclear industry.

Aside from these criticisms, he enjoyed working there — particularly the informal atmosphere and the autonomy afforded him by his position. There was not much latitude in what was to be done. As Norm had emphasized, "there is no discretion." But he had a lot of freedom in how to go about doing it.

Professional disagreements were usually aired and resolved through the chain of command. Although he had never been involved in serious disagreements with colleagues or clients before, he knew from talking with other engineers that Atomic Engineering was supportive of field staff who encountered difficulties with host organization personnel. He decided that his life and career were just about where he wanted them. Soon he would probably receive a promotion, especially since he had just received a letter of commendation from Neubauer.

Robert had taken the time to express his thanks and appreciation for the excellent quality of Jeff's work and the cooperative relationships that Jeff had established with clients over the past year. Jeff hoped that today's events would not affect this friendship.

It was now nine o'clock and starting to rain. He was glad that he had ordered room service earlier. Jeff really did not want to go out, but felt he had spent too much time alone in hotel rooms and unfamiliar places. The fact that he lived away from his home and family so much of the time, he surmised, was one personal factor behind his decision to question the industry. When he was at home in Michigan, he was always too busy with the kids or other obligations to keep abreast of current engineering reports and studies. The leisure recently given him to read had started him thinking.

TREADING DEEP WATER

Last year he began to receive assignments that took him to a variety of regions throughout the United States. On these trips he enjoyed free time to read. There was not much else to do. He came across articles and books critical of nuclear plant safety. This new perspective was very different from the one he shared with his engineering colleagues. Jeff decided to delve more deeply into the literature and began to look at the industry with a more critical eye. When he discussed his criticisms with his colleagues, he was met with resistance. The general feeling among them was "Don't make waves." They felt that the industry would solve most of its problems and that policy concerns should be left to the executives and experts. It began to dawn on him that most of the people with whom he worked defined their roles narrowly and were unconcerned with bothersome ethical questions.

During this period in the mid-1970s, the nuclear industry was suffering chronic delays and shutdowns. Jeff decided to focus his thoughts on the problem. He discussed his ideas for a paper with Robert Neubauer and Norm Lawrence. Norm asked him to work with William Seymour, an environmental specialist. Seymour would help him prepare a paper for publication by the *Journal of Nuclear News* and assist in getting the paper cleared through Atomic Engineering.

The paper was to emphasize that the nuclear industry had allowed its management philosophy to lag behind its technical development and that centralized procedures should be implemented to correct the resulting safety problems. Jeff also planned to argue for the standardization of nuclear plants. Each new plant was custom designed for the host organization. There were no directives from the AEC to institute uniform designs. Standardization would ultimately mean increased safety and reliability and would make the licensing procedures less complicated. In his view it offered every conceivable advantage. He hoped to be able to highlight the disparity without having to cite his own experience with Atomic Engineering.

As it turned out, his own experiences were the only data he had, or could get. His literature search yielded few discussions on the quality of nuclear plant management. By June he had finished his initial draft and prepared an abstract that was approved by the *Journal of Nuclear News*. He was assigned to Baltimore Utility Corporation (BUCORP) in Maryland at that time. Jeff was to assist in developing a comprehensive QA program for a new nuclear generating plant.

While there, Jeff contacted an old navy friend, US Rep. Patrick O'Conner. He wanted Patrick to read his paper and to become more informed about a topic that would grow in importance in the years ahead. At the same time, Jeff started to doubt his idea that "reform" was the answer to the problem. Through personal contacts and his experiences at Atomic Engineering, he began to recognize that the real problem might be the type of people who worked for the nuclear industry. There were not enough first-rate engineers and executives, like those employed by BUCORP.

Jeff became confirmed in this opinion in September while working at BUCORP. Jeff happened to read a copy of a memo written by a BUCORP engineer. The memo mentioned that there were still serious design problems in several containment systems two years after they were released for marketing. The industry was apparently cutting corners, trying to get nuclear plants sold, licensed, and running while disregarding safety. Another related problem identified in the memo was inadequate prototype testing — it was being conducted *after* nuclear systems were marketed. QA was also inadequate because third party inspections of component systems were not required and nuclear plant managers and staff generally regarded QA with resignation and suspicion.

Jeff began to feel that the major reason for the current situation was the corporate structure of the industry. The highest level of management, as in other major corporations, was dominated by sales, marketing, and fiscal specialists. The industry's standard practice was "sell first, test later." He became increasingly disturbed as he realized that there was a reasonable doubt about the safety of nuclear plants inside and outside the United States.

In mid-September, Representative O'Conner received a copy of Jeff's final paper, which criticized the nuclear industry. Jeff was disappointed shortly thereafter when he received word that Patrick considered personal action on his part out of the question. It seemed that this was a politically sensitive issue that, if pursued, could seriously damage his political ambitions. Jeff originally thought that Patrick would sponsor legislation that would remedy some of these problems. Disappointed with Patrick's reaction, Jeff decided to forward a copy of his paper to Bruce Arnold, an active lobbyist against nuclear power usage. Just a few days earlier he had seen Bruce on a local television show, debating the safety of nuclear plants.

Bruce enthusiastically read the paper. It was an important document written by someone still *within* the industry. Most dissidents were "former this" or "former that" who, once they were fired or resigned, lost their credibility in the eyes of the public. Within a few days Bruce called Jeff to ask if he could include the paper in the upcoming US Senate proceedings. Jeff was elated: he would have a second chance to alert Congress. One question remained: Who would present it?

The hearing was only two weeks away, and Bruce knew from experience that unless someone was adequately prepared to undergo rigorous questioning, his testimony would not be credible. Jeff lacked the expertise. After discussing it, they jointly decided to have Jeff's paper appended to Bruce's testimony. After all, Jeff was not interested in recognition or glory — he only wanted the public to be aware of these problems. For his purposes, who presented it would be irrelevant.

While back in Michigan the next week for a series of seminars, Jeff showed Seymour the paper. Seymour stressed that it was a controversial subject but did not question the validity of the facts. His only concern was for the effect it would have on Jeff's career if published. He suggested that the paper be rewritten. Jeff did not mention that the wheels were already in motion for its release next week at the hearings.

From Jeff's perspective, too many of his colleagues were content to ignore such global problems. They hoped that they could deal with their jobs in a noncontroversial, efficient way, get promoted, and retire in 20 years, unencumbered by problematic concerns. However, he was not content to accept a similar role. His professional obligations encompassed more than just doing a "good job."

At times he almost envied their complacency. He was treading deep water — no other line engineer had publicly criticized the industry, and he feared that by talking in broad policy terms his action would be interpreted as some kind of organizational disloyalty. No one had spelled out a code of ethics for line engineers who were addressing public policy issues. There were no precedents and his only guidelines were his own.

ALL IS NOT WELL

Jeff awoke the following morning to the sound of his alarm clock. He was anxious to return to work at BUCORP after spending the previous week in training. Several days later Jeff received the telephone call. "Get back here on the next plane!" his project manager had said. "Norm has been getting calls from all over the country about your paper." Jeff was able to book a flight for later that evening. Once he had cleared his desk, he returned to the hotel to pack. The phone call had made him a bit nervous.

The cool reception he received the next morning did not allay his fears. He asked himself: "Am I being paranoid or are most of my associates acting as though they don't know me?" On the way to Norm's office, Robert barely acknowledged him.

After a few minutes the secretary said, "Mr. Lawrence will see you now." There he sat, just as Jeff had imagined. Norm never looked comfortable in a three-piece suit. The style of clothes that he had initially worn — dress slacks and casual shirts — had made him seem more an engineer than a corporate executive, but over the years Norm had removed himself from the engineering mainstream, preferring to devote his energies to building an internationally recognized corporation. In a short period of time he had made substantial progress. He motioned for Jeff to sit down. No greetings were exchanged. Norm was the first to speak.

Norm: Jeff, I have received at least ten phone calls from irate clients. They were complaining about your Senate paper. What the hell is going on?

Jeff: I spoke to you about some of my concerns regarding the industry several months ago. At that time I was working on an initial draft of a paper that would encompass these doubts. Since then I've . . .

Norm: I remember the conversation, but as I recall that was for publication with the *Journal of Nuclear News*, not for a U.S. Senate hearing! Jeff, you've been with us long enough to know that all planned publications have to be cleared through Atomic Engineering. That policy guideline would certainly include papers presented before a congressional committee. William tells me that he told you to rewrite your IES paper. Right?

Jeff: That's right. He did suggest that I revise it, and I will if the data and reasoning warrant it, but . . .

Norm: You're damn right they warrant it! I've reviewed your paper and so have several other people here. We question the judgment drawn from the facts that you reference. Yesterday I spoke with several people whom you reference. Do you want to know what they said? All of them disagree with *your* analysis of *their* data. We simply believe that your paper is not quantitatively or qualitatively correct in the technical sense.

Jeff: I strongly disagree, Norm! I've been over and over the data. I've done my homework and it all checks out. Pressure from the industry has made people modify and dilute their original data. Out in the field I've come across problems on nuclear safety that take precedence over Atomic Engineering, over my career, over corporate and industry profits, all the way down the line. Surely as an engineer, you can understand that I have an obligation to protect the public, and as a citizen I have a right to voice these concerns. That's all I am doing. The paper that was entered into the *Congressional Record* is a version of the *Nuclear News* article. I wrote it as a private citizen, not as an employee of Atomic Engineering! Atomic Engineering is not even mentioned. Entering something into the record at a congressional hearing as a private citizen is a lot different than publishing something in a national engineering journal.

Norm: An engineer doesn't write up his thesis of a job he's doing and put it into the public record without approval from the company. You got your experience through Atomic Engineering and therefore anything you publish belongs to Atomic Engineering! You've taken the work of others, which is substantiated and indicated one thing, and changed the emphasis and interpretation to vitiate completely what they have done. You've then arrived at a different solution but still referenced their work and implied that they agree. Distortions of this kind, Jeff, do not indicate good engineering judgment. Whether explicitly or implicitly, you've also referenced proprietary information that belongs to our clients. It is our policy and the policy of any reputable consulting firm to honor client confidences. Over and over it has been stressed that we should maintain the proprietary rights of clients for whom we work. We're not an investigating company. Moreover, it seems to me that you shouldn't want to work within the very industry that you're criticizing.

Jeff: I made my decision to speak out without resigning because people would listen to me then. I am an employee of the nuclear industry and as such I would have credibility. Norm, the industry needs to be reformed, not destroyed. Of course, I realize that I am in a catch-22 situation where my credibility turns on my relationship with the industry, even though the industry might not want me employed after they've heard what I have to say. I don't believe that I've done anything that could be construed as unethical. If anything, I've fulfilled my obligation as an engineer to protect the public interest. I'm not arguing for the shutdown of nuclear plants — I just think there are problems within the industry that need to be addressed. No one else is addressing them and we're running out of time. Is it going to take a catastrophic nuclear accident to force the industry to implement the needed reforms? As far as not protecting proprietary information, I didn't disclose any specific information that could be traced to a particular client. It's true that my paper was based on my experiences with different nuclear power plants' managements, but how else would I make my points if not allowed to discuss that experience? The paper addresses broad policy matters and recommends legislative remedies. It doesn't accuse any particular client of wrongdoing.

Norm: We contacted the committee concerning the errors contained in your paper. Although it's too late to correct the record, it is not too late to amend your *Nuclear News* article — to set the record straight. As a personal favor to me, I want you to revise it. I can tell you right now that I will not approve it for publication in its present state. The points that you're trying to make are not substantiated by the data. By changing the interpretation, you have disregarded the original authors' intentions. Until you revise it, I will not even consider giving you my approval. I think that's about all the time I have to discuss this matter. As of right now I'm taking you off the BUCORP project. I want you to report to Robert. He'll give you your new assignment. That's all.

Jeff: I will reevaluate the paper, but I'd like to continue this discussion. I do have a few more things I'd like to say.

Norm: Sorry, Jeff, I have another appointment.

With that concluding comment, Norm summoned his secretary. His tone of voice alerted her to "be on her toes." All was not well, as was also evidenced by Jeff's expression when he walked out the door, and by the letter of dismissal he received five days later. The reason stated: failure to safeguard proprietary materials.

Jeff felt that there was no alternative for him. One week later, to generate support, he sent copies of the paper to the *New York Times*, the *Washington Post*, and various senators and congressmen. Copies of nuclear operating reports and the memorandums substantiating his concerns were also released. He was thankful that he had made copies.

During the next several months, it was evident that his paper had effected no significant industry reforms. Congress had ignored his recommendations. Congressional immunities were even denied him owing to a technicality. Within a few weeks of his firing he had contacted the Justice Department to state his belief that his dismissal was a violation of Title 18, Section 1505 of the US Code, which protects congressional witnesses from reprisal. No protection was forthcoming because he had not been subpoenaed but rather had made his views voluntarily known.

The fear that his concerns would go unheeded led him to invoke the media as an alternative strategy. He expected them to pick up where Congress left off and to do some muckraking to ascertain how badly the industry was being managed. Again, he was disappointed. Almost no media coverage ensued.

Although the public was still unaware of the risks of nuclear power, because of this lack of attention in the press, he believed that his actions had not been totally in vain. The companies that marketed the defective systems suffered a marked drop in sales after the release of his paper.

At the same time that these events were unfolding, Jeff was actively trying to secure employment. He submitted more than 43 job applications to corporations in technical fields; only 1 responded. "We have a job open in Argentina," the personnel director had said. Jeff declined.

He had obtained a job as a recreational director at a local YMCA by the time his unemployment benefits expired. After months of closed doors and unanswered letters, he knew that he had been blackballed from his chosen profession.

RECENT EVENTS

Since Jeff's dismissal, other nuclear engineers have stepped forward with similar accusations, and a number of studies have substantiated his concerns about plant safety. The partial meltdown at the Three Mile Island nuclear plant has vindicated Jeff and others who have spoken out. The nuclear industry has subsequently suffered dozens of plant postponements and cancellations of orders. A recent study, done for the Nuclear Regulatory Commission by the Oak Ridge National Laboratory, concluded that the accident at Three Mile Island Unit 2 was just 1 of 141 mishaps that had the potential to lead to a meltdown.[1] Jeff now believes that

> It is events, not people, who ultimately change things in society. The individual citizen does not count for anything. There just aren't enough forces mobilized behind an individual citizen to have it count for anything on Capitol Hill — no matter how good his ideas are, or how knowledgeable he is, or how many documents he has to back up his stand. Under no circumstances has Congress ever listened to a private citizen, acted on that private citizen's recommendations, and developed a program for legislative reform based on his suggestions. It just doesn't happen. The things that will change society are events first, followed by people who previously blew the whistle who are brought forward by the media as "I told you so."

THE ETHICS OF WHISTLEBLOWING

Jeff Thomas is a "classic" case of a whistleblower. His experiences readily serve to illustrate the personal and professional dilemmas that can confront an individual, and just as readily the arguments for and against the various courses of action available.

The Duty of Loyalty

Norm Lawrence, his employer, strongly opposes Jeff's decision to go public. He believes that an employee's primary obligation is to his employer and that whistleblowing is a breach of this obligation. Although he says little or nothing in defense of his view, one can easily construct one.

The main argument is contractual. As an employee, one enters into an agreement with one's employer to perform certain services in return for certain payments. Implicit in the contract, Norm would contend, is a commitment of confidentiality. Such a commitment is necessary in order to make the relationship workable. Just as an individual has a right to privacy, so do corporations, and a corporation can expect that those who enter into contractual relationships with it will respect this right to privacy.

The difficulty with any such contractarian approach is that it is excessively legalistic and purely formal. As a result it is insensitive to the exceptions that would justify breach of contract. All of us recognize conditions under which an individual must be freed from the terms of a contract — when he or she is unable to satisfy the terms or perhaps when some other contract takes precedence.

Jeff believed that his obligation of loyalty to his employer was overridden by his obligation of loyalty to society. The threat of a nuclear accident is very serious, the harm that would be done is too extensive, and the probability of its occurrence too high for silence to be warranted.

Internal versus External Dissent

Norm concedes a right of dissent, while denying a right to blow the whistle, because he recognizes a right of external dissent: one can criticize the organization from the outside. What he denies is the right to criticize the organization while one is still a member of it. In his view Jeff should have resigned; he would then have been free to voice his concerns. As a citizen at large, he could raise whatever objections he chose against the nuclear industry. But, according to Norm, he should not enjoy this privilege as long as he remains an employee within it.

Why not? The answer may again be in terms of loyalty: in return for one's livelihood one owes one's employer confidentiality. But where would such an obligation come from? It is not part of the explicit contract. Indeed, it is difficult to read it into an implicit contract. For insofar as one is hired as an engineer, one is bound by the engineers' code of professional conduct. This code explicitly requires engineers to put public safety ahead of profits and other private or indeed personal concerns. One could then argue just as easily that the implied terms of the contract require one to blow the whistle when the safety of the public is threatened.

Responsible Dissent

Richard DeGeorge argues that specific conditions must be satisfied before dissent outside the organization is warranted.[2]

Barring exceptional circumstances, an individual must first try to change things from within the organization. In Jeff's case, since it was not just his employer but the entire industry on which he sought to blow the whistle, this requirement would be difficult to satisfy. But certainly Jeff had alerted some of his superiors to his concerns: he had discussed his paper with them, and he let them know of his intention to publish it.

Second, an individual must try to verify his or her claims. Jeff had done this. He had checked out his facts and gathered data from others to substantiate them; so he was not making reckless charges but documented allegations.

Third, the issue must be serious. Blowing the whistle on trivia unnecessarily disrupts the workplace and prevents one from getting on with the job. Professional dissent would then become backbiting and gossiping. Jeff's concerns, however, were serious. A meltdown could cause death and destruction of unique proportions, and the risk of it happening was unnecessarily high, in Jeff's professional judgment.

Consequently, the case can easily be made that Jeff's actions constituted responsible dissent: he voiced his concerns, checked out his facts, and then dealt with a serious threat.

Procedural Justice

Jeff's strategy differed from that of others: he went to Congress. However, he was not forced to testify — he had not received a subpoena. He went voluntarily. Moreover, he did not testify in person but had his paper presented by a third party.

Those who testify in person are protected from retaliation. Technically, Jeff did not have this protection. So, when he was subsequently fired from his job, he was unsuccessful in invoking congressional immunity. Was procedural justice done?

Few are likely to place much weight in the technicality on which the Department of Justice dismissed Jeff's petition. Yet his case does raise a serious question: How far should such immunity extend? Should it cover those who are cited in Jeff's paper? Should it cover those who provide data or documents to congressional committees? If one finds fault with the technicality, one must begin to address these questions.

GUIDE QUESTIONS

1. Are the problems Jeff addresses ones that concern personnel, management, technical, or political issues?
2. As consultants to the nuclear industry, can an organization like Atomic Engineering effectively address the problem that Jeff discusses?
3. What other options, if any, were available to Jeff?
4. Jeff does not regret blowing the whistle, but if you were he, would you?
5. Was Jeff foolish to do what he did?
6. Would you have agreed to revise your paper?
7. Do you think Norm is right in saying that Jeff should have resigned first?
8. If you were Norm and had received ten telephone calls from irate clients, what would you have done with Jeff?
9. How far should immunity be extended to whistleblowers in relationship to congressional hearings?
10. Should Congress protect people who author papers and subsequently have them read into the *Record* by someone else?
11. Is Jeff naive in thinking that Congress can provide a remedy?
12. How much responsibility for safe nuclear power should reside with engineers, as opposed to management or government regulatory agencies?

NOTES

1. Matthew L. Wald. "US Study Reassesses Risk of Nuclear Plant Accidents," *New York Times*, July 6, 1982, p. A10.
2. Richard De George. "Ethical Responsibilities of Engineers in Large Organizations: The Pinto Case" (Paper presented at the National Conference on Engineering Ethics, Rensselaer Polytechnic Institute, Troy, NY, June 20–22, 1980).

SUGGESTED READINGS

Beetle, George R. "Engineering and Society: A Contemporary Challenge." *Civil Engineering* 41 (February 1971): 51–53.

Bogen, Kenneth T. "Managing Technical Dissent in Private Industry: Societal and Corporate Strategies for Dealing with the Whistle-blowing Professional." *Industrial and Labor Relations Forum* 13 (1979): 3–32.

Fluegge, Ronald M. "Whistle-blowing and Scientific Responsibility: The Management of Technical Dissent." Paper presented at the 144th National Meeting of the American Association for the Advancement of Science, Washington, DC, February 12–17, 1978.

Ford, Daniel. "A Reporter at Large: Three Mile Island." pt.1. *New Yorker*, April 6, 1981, pp. 49–120.

———. "A Reporter at Large: Three Mile Island." pt.2. *New Yorker*, April 13, 1981, pp. 46–108.

Hirshman, Albert L. *Exit, Voice, and Loyalty*. Cambridge, Mass.: Harvard University Press, 1970.

Pollard, Robert D., ed. *The Nugget File*. Cambridge, Mass.: Union of Concerned Scientists, 1979.

Rashke, Richard. *The Killing of Karen Silkwood: The Story behind the Kerr-McGee Plutonium Case.* Boston, Mass.: Houghton Mifflin, 1981.

"The San Jose Three." *Time* February 16, 1976, p. 78.

Solomon, Lewis, and Terry Garcia. "Protecting the Corporate Whistle Blower under Federal Anti-Retaliation Statutes." *Journal of Corporation Law* 5 (Winter 1980): 275–297.

Union of Concerned Scientists. *Testimony of Bridenbaugh, Hubbard, and Minor before the JCAE.* February 18, 1976. Cambridge, Mass.: Union of Concerned Scientists, 1976.

Weil, Vivian. "The Browns Ferry Case." In *Conflicting Loyalties in the Workplace,* edited by F. A. Elliston. Notre Dame, Ind.: University of Notre Dame Press, forthcoming.

Welch, B. L. "Deception on Nuclear Power Risks: A Call for Action." *Bulletin of the Atomic Scientists* 36 (September 1980): 50–54.

PART THREE
LESSONS
LEARNED

TEN
SOME
RECOMMENDATIONS

FOR INDIVIDUALS

There are a number of important recommendations for individuals who are considering blowing the whistle. The simplest and most important lesson to learn is: Be careful! The decision to blow the whistle is not one to be taken lightly. Professionally, it can cost an employee not only his or her job but also a career. Personally, it can cost much grief — disrupted sleep, strained friendships, and diminished fortunes. Those who decide to dissent publicly should recognize that they are gambling, and the odds are against them.

They should realize that it is a lonely lot they are choosing, and they will receive little help from others. The stigma of being called a "whistleblower" ostracizes the individual from colleagues at work and other members of their professions. And even though they may be treated unfairly, they will typically find that they have little recourse through institutional channels like the courts, Congress, or professional associations.

Responsible whistleblowing has its own lessons. First, the individual is less likely to suffer if he or she has the facts straight: verification of any empirical claims is important for both moral and prudential reasons. Second, the whistleblower should try to resolve his or her differences within the organization before going outside it. The traditional demands of loyalty will be met if one first tries to change matters from within. It will also be less trouble and troublesome — perhaps allowing matters to be resolved quickly. And finally, the prospects are frequently better for effecting changes within the organization, among colleagues who are known and familiar with the problems.

At the practical level the whistleblower should realize that there are many ways to dissent. It is important that he or she be aware of the full range of options open and weigh the alternatives carefully. The individual can go to the press, leak information to community action groups, seek redress through the courts, use the Office of Inspectors General, appeal to professional societies, or go to Congress. Each strategy has advantages and disadvantages, depending on the specifics of the situation. One of the lessons from this project is the appropriateness of different alternatives.

If an individual has tried working within the system and meets resistance that cannot be overcome, he or she should recognize that a decision to blow the whistle can be examined as a meritorious human action based on sincerity, commitment, and self-sacrifice. A serious problem that could have led to harmful damages to other people might have otherwise continued had the whistle not been blown. Like the self-sacrificing soldier on the field of battle, the whistleblower sacrifices himself or herself for the "company." Although the person most likely will suffer abuse and ridicule, at least the individual can rest easy that he has followed his or her conscience and can avoid the feelings of guilt a whistleblower would otherwise suffer.

There are no clear and simple guidelines that can be offered to the potential whistleblower. The choice is a difficult one with good and bad features associated with each alternative. A careful assessment of these alternatives and their costs would at least give the whistleblower a more enlightened perspective and a firmer basis for rational choice.

FOR ORGANIZATIONS

There are a number of important recommendations for organizations concerning whistleblowing. The following discussion is especially appropriate for chief executive officers (CEOs) and upper-level managers.

Personal Characteristics of Whistleblowers

Organizations need to become more aware of the personal traits of whistleblowers. Typically organizations conceive of such people as "troublemakers," dissatisfied and ineffective employees who are unable to work within the system. Or worse, they are considered downright "traitors."

An empirical study of whistleblowers dispels this myth. They run the gamut of organizational stereotypes — from the vocal publicity hound to the meek bureaucrat. Many are among the most dedicated and committed employees in the organization. They often possess high personal standards and are sensitive to threats to the welfare of individuals inside or outside the organization. Ultimately, they decide to blow the whistle in frustration because of a perceived lack of understanding, support, or opportunity to resolve problems from within.

Management should be sensitive to the unexpected problems that can arise when they decide to make an example of the individual. If their goal is to discourage whistleblowing, demoting, penalizing, or firing the person will certainly get that message across to other employees. But this strategy can easily create resentment and antagonism among loyal and sympathetic workers. By lashing back management risks hostile feelings in other employees, even those who would otherwise remain loyal and supportive to the company. This strategy also tends to create a martyr image of the whistleblower in the public at large. The organization thereby risks becoming another corporate bad guy — a bully abusing the conscientious and innocent little guy. The long-term results can be a tarnished reputation with hidden penalties in the form of withdrawn public support, reduced sales, or boycotts.

Organizations should approach the problem with a different tack. Since whistleblowing occurs when the internal mechanisms for resolving complaints are weak or nonexistent,[1] management should create internal avenues for dissent. If an employee has these available, he or she has less need to go outside the organization for a fair hearing of complaints. If the potential whistleblower is a dedicated and highly principled employee, as many are, the individual will not embarrass the company by washing their dirty linen in public.

Management should recognize that human perception is selective and each person sees corporate life from a different perspective. For example, each manager and professional tends to perceive those aspects of a situation as it relates specifically to his or her personal goals or to those of his or her co-workers or department.[2] The same principle applies to the various beliefs about whether or not blowing the whistle is justified.

These differences in perception should be dealt with through some mediating mechanism within the organization. Giving the potential whistleblower an opportunity to share his or her concerns allows the person to recognize that the organization does care about the "correct" course of action, the fair, and the just policy. In a trusting and open environment, such differences can be discussed and opportunities provided for compromise and adjustment.[3] The potential whistleblower is thereby given the opportunity to discover whether he or she is correct or incorrect in factual assessment and can be informed of the rationale for decisions by management. Management, in turn, has an opportunity to have mistaken assumptions underlying corporate policy disclosed and corrected and to become clearer on the unanticipated consequences of its actions. The potential whistleblower might lack important information since he or she does not have access to all the information available to management. On the other hand, management often lacks equally important information that the potential whistleblower possesses, because he or she is a specialist with professional expertise and privileged information and skills acquired through education and work experience. By providing mechanisms within the organization for sharing perceptions, pooling information, and conducting informal arbitration, management can better avoid the undesirable effects of whistleblowing in the organization. This strategy would simultaneously enhance the flow of information, facilitate communication, and enhance organizational effectiveness.

Organizational Roles

But of this research come a number of important recommendations concerning the assignment of tasks within the organization. Organizations can be treated as systems of roles that ideally interrelate in a smooth fashion in accomplishing organizational goals. Often, however, interrole conflicts occur, and out of such conflicts the seeds for whistleblowing grow. These conflicts are not rooted in the personality of the individuals but in their conflicting assignments and responsibilities. These role conflicts are of two sorts: intrarole conflict, which occurs because irreconcilable demands are placed on one role; and interrole conflict, which occurs when two roles are incompatible within one network.

A major source of interrole conflict can be resolved through (1) the separation of task-specialist roles and managerial roles and (2) the development of mechanisms within the organization to reconcile the competing demands of each. Task specialists are professionals hired because of their knowledge and expertise gained through their prior educational and work experience. Their primary work goal is to accomplish specific tasks related to their area of expertise. The managerial role, on the other hand, is to act as an overseer concerned with the coordination of the various tasks that specialists perform. The manager's goal is to supervise and control the functioning of a variety of specialists in order to attain larger organizational goals. These two roles are subject to different and occasionally conflicting demands. When the role is played by one individual, interrole conflict can lead to whistleblowing. If the roles are separated, if the tasks are performed by different individuals, and if mechanisms are introduced to reconcile their conflicting demands in a mutually satisfactory manner, whistleblowing is less likely.

Organizations should develop means whereby their task specialists and managers can share their different views and recognize their conflicting objectives in an open, trusting environment. At times the specialist must understand the necessity to make compromises or indeed sacrifices in terms of his or her task goals. The individual must recognize his or her role as also being that of an employee who is expected to cooperate and work toward larger organizational goals. But when the task specialist raises technical concerns that involve potentially dangerous effects, managerial role players should defer to the more reliable judgment of their subordinates, at least until these matters are properly investigated to determine the facts, the risks, and the appropriate course of action. To insist upon unquestioning "obedience" at such times pushes the specialist into an uncomfortable intrarole conflict. This employee is pulled in two mutually exclusive directions: either to be a loyal employee and follow orders or to remain committed to the standards and principles of his or her profession. Whistleblowing is the result of this conflict when the professional elects to defer to his or her professional code and conscience.

Organizations should try to ensure that both managers and task specialists are informed about such role conflicts. If they are recognized beforehand, the tendency to react by labeling the problem as a "personality difference" would be held in check, and the roots of the conflict can be addressed. The individuals can more effectively seek means to avoid a conflict situation, which provides for no outlet short of someone's transfer, demotion, or firing. These conflict situations can cost the organizations valuable human resources, and leave the source of the problem unattended. Organizations need clearly defined means for recognizing and addressing differences of opinion that arise out of role conflicts. Managers and task specialists should be given training in diagnosing such conflicts and developing effective strategies for resolving them.[4]

Anonymous Whistleblowing

Employees face a difficult choice in raising their concerns publicly. Members of the organization want to appear to others, especially outside the organization, in a favorable light. They may therefore be tempted to cover up or ignore important issues. The short-term gain is a smoothly functioning organization. The long-term results can bode ill for the welfare of the organization and its members. Some individuals facing such a dilemma may choose to blow the whistle anonymously — because they fear the sanctions that would be brought against them by their organization as the result of publicity and recognition.

To avoid anonymous whistleblowing organizations should provide channels for anonymously dissenting within the organization. Such channels should be accessible to all and should ensure an investigation of serious allegations and appropriate remedial actions. Without such channels, the potential whistleblower will be forced to go outside the organization to raise his or her concerns.

Organizational Systems and Controls

Organizations should recognize that the more democratic and participative their control system and the more open and trusting their environments, the less whistleblowing is likely to occur.[5] When organizations tend toward authoritarian-coercive control systems, they foster a rigidity and lack of flexibility to respond to internal conflicts.[6] In such situations, potential whistleblowers feel incapable of moving the bureaucracy and are forced to go outside it.

The more hierarchical and centralized their control systems, the more individuals feel alienated and the more difficult it will be for them to raise ethical issues and concerns. Information becomes increasingly distorted the more channels it must pass through. Moving to less hierarchical and more decentralized control systems allows for greater flexibility and more opportunity for nonconfrontational dialogue.

If organizations cannot or do not desire to move toward this type of control system, whistleblowing will be an ever-present possibility. Short of democratization of the workplace, management should seriously consider formal or informal mechanisms by which their employees can raise ethical issues and concerns in a satisfactory manner so as to reduce the number of potential whistleblowing situations from arising.

Organizational Culture

All organizations possess a corporate and managerial culture that emphasizes certain values and norms. The corporate culture is greatly influenced by the CEO and top management. When the leadership within the organization engages in, sanctions, or overlooks unethical and questionable practices in order to achieve corporate goals, those lower in the organization get the message. For example, a recent survey of managers at Pitney-Bowes, the Stamford, Connecticut, manufacturer of business equipment and a recognized leader in corporate ethics, indicated that a majority of them feel pressure to compromise personal ethics to achieve corporate goals. These results are similar to a study at Uniroyal, the $2.2 billion rubber and plastics company, whose officers felt pressure to compromise personal ethics and corporate goals. Some 61 percent of Pitney-Bowes's managers and 54 percent of Uniroyal's managers would not refuse orders to market off-standard and possibly dangerous items.[7]

When top management emphasizes economic efficiency and accountability, growth, and loyalty to the company, to the exclusion of ethical values and social responsibilities, they open the door for whistleblowing. Management should realize that whistleblowers have high ideals that extend beyond their organization. Management can attempt to "weed out" such idealists and label them trouble-makers. Rarely, however, can an organization totally eliminate dissent through such tactics. Just one employee can blow the whistle and ruin a company's carefully cultivated image. Management would do well to change the corporate culture by placing greater importance on reporting unethical and questionable practices within the organization. Rhetoric is not enough: management needs to develop a reward system that effectively encourages such behavior.

Organizational Size, Technology, and Change

The larger the organization and the more technologically complex the task environment, the more an organization is susceptible to whistleblowing. This occurs because of the inherent inertia and rigidity of large-scale, complex organizations. The whistleblower attempts to change the behavior or activities of individuals inside of the organization in some manner and feels compelled to go outside when he or she has exhausted all internal procedures. Organizations should provide means of dissent that channel the good intentions of loyal employees in constructive directions. This recommendation applies to all kinds of organizations but holds especially true for large-scale organizations with technologically complex work environments.

James Thompson offers several worthwhile suggestions. These include increasing employee professionalization, forming a looser structure, decentralizing authority, creating freer communications, developing project organization, rotating assignments, using group processes, restructuring continually, implementing a different incentive system, and introducing a variety of other changes in management practices.[8] Rensis Likert has provided a means of assessing the organization's internal health,[9] suggesting strategies for moving an organization closer to the "ideal" system where there is a participative and democratic leadership system with a great deal of confidence and trust being shown in subordinates. Individuals are typically motivated by rewards and involvement, and communication flows down, up, and sideways. Decisions are made throughout the entire organization, and except in crisis situations, goal getting is by group action. Review functions are widely shared throughout the organization. Whistleblowing might be expected to be much less probably in such an organization.

The Organization and Its Environment

Organizations must adapt to their environments if they are to survive. With the continued acceleration of change, adaptation is becoming more difficult. Changes in technology, the economy, government regulations, consumer preferences, work patterns, and media coverage are occurring rapidly and require that organizations become more involved with forecasting changes before they occur. Whistleblowing can be taken as an attempt at warning the organization of some undesirable changes in its environment that might arise if certain adaptations are not made.

Accordingly, organizations should take a more proactive approach to the whistleblowing problem by seeking out a variety of perceptions of present or possible future difficulties that relate to illegal, dangerous, or unethical behavior. By gathering such information, organizations can reduce whistleblowing. This may require making adjustments to the entire organizational system. As West Churchman suggests, improving systems depends upon understanding the properties of the whole system, and the problem of system improvement is a problem of the "ethics of the whole system."[10]

Rigid conformity to past practices seriously handicaps organizations, making them inflexible and unresponsive to new approaches. Greater flexibility and openness will reduce whistleblowing problems and improve the prospects for organizational survival. Failure to adapt to their changing environment will most likely lead to an increase in whistleblowing as changing environments place increasing pressure on organizations.

SUMMARY

This charge has presented several important recommendations to individuals who are considering blowing the whistle. Recommendations have also been made to organizations concerned with understanding and dealing with whistleblowing more effectively. Issues explored in this chapter include such topics as the personal characteristics and traits of whistleblowers, organizational roles, anonymous whistleblowing, organizational systems and controls, organizational culture, and organizational size, technology, and change.

NOTES

1. See Chapter 1.
2. DeWitt C. Dearborn and Herbert A. Simon, "Selective Perception: A Note on the Departmental Identification of Executives," *Sociometry* 21 (1958): 140–144.
3. Michael Doctoroff, *Synergistic Management: Creating the Climate for Superior Performance* (New York: AMACOM, 1977).
4. Robert Bolton, *People Skills* (Englewood Cliffs, NJ: Prentice-Hall, 1979).
5. American Institute of CPAs, *Tentative Report of the Special Advisory Committee on Internal Control*, New York, September 15, 1978, pp. 9–12.
6. Rensis Likert, *The Human Organization: Its Management and Value* (New York: McGraw-Hill, 1967).
7. "The Pressure to Compromise Personal Ethics," *Business Week*, January 31, 1977, p. 107.
8. James P. Thompson, ed., *Approaches to Organizational Design* (Pittsburgh: University of Pittsburgh Press, 1966).
9. Likert, *The Human Organization.*
10. West Churchman, *Challenge to Reason* (New York: McGraw-Hill, 1968).

APPENDIX
THE LITERATURE

THE LITERARY TRADITION

Within the last decade increased attention has been given to the responsibilities of professionals toward their employers, colleagues, and the public. As a result there is a growing body of literature in professional ethics that specifically addresses the topic of dissent or *whistleblowing,* as it is commonly termed.

A variety of whistleblowers have written about their own experiences in order to inform would-be whistleblowers of the dangers or to make the public aware of some potential threat. Several authors have focused on the historical or economic facets of whistleblowing, whereas others have approached it from a political or scientific perspective. Philosophers have examined its moral and ethical aspects, and legal scholars have explored the rights of employees to disclose wrongdoing and the protections they are afforded against retaliation. The literature covers the gamut from popular accounts to scholarly analyses.

Popular Materials

Popular materials consist mainly of personal guidance books and articles and individual accounts by or about whistleblowers. Among these, a few are noteworthy and deserve attention.

One of the more informative self-help books for public employees is *A Whistleblower's Guide to the Federal Bureaucracy,* published by the Government Accountability Project (GAP).[1] Using past cases of whistleblowing as examples, it addresses the timing, method, and probability of success for whistleblowing; how not to blow the whistle; and pathways through the bureaucracy. In "How to Whistle," Peter Broida reviews the process of registering a complaint under the Civil Service Reform Act, which is designed to protect whistleblowers.[2]

For employees in the private sector, Tekla Perry offers eight suggestions for potential whistleblowers in "Knowing How to Blow the Whistle,"[3] as does Peter Raven-Hansen in "Do and Don'ts for Whistleblowing."[4]

Individual accounts written by whistleblowers also enlighten one as to possible perils and pitfalls. In "The High Cost of Whistleblowing," Paul Matteucci discusses his eight years spent trying to convince his employer that America's missile warning system was dangerously inadequate.[5] Kermit Vandivier's article, "The Aircraft Brake Scandal," chronicles his dilemma at the B.F. Goodrich Company.[6] Ernest Fitzgerald, the most well-known whistleblower, writes of his ordeals after he testified before Congress about the $2 billion cost overrun on the C-5A cargo plane.[7] The book is a well-documented study of mismanagement and inefficiency in the federal bureaucracy.

Several books fall into this self-help category but go one step further. In addition to presenting whistleblower accounts, they offer a number of recommendations and analyses. For example, in *Whistle-blowing*, Ralph Nader, Pete Petkas, and Kate Blackwell supplement their 11 stories with recommendations and suggestions that evolved out of a conference on professional responsibility.[8] Alan Westin presents 10 autobiographical accounts in *Whistleblowing: Loyalty and Dissent in the Corporation*.[9] His opening chapter provides an explanation for the increase in whistleblowing, whereas his concluding chapter focuses on what can and should be done to protect whistleblowers in industry.

Individual accounts written about whistleblowers are also quite popular. *Divided Loyalties*, the first of its kind, offers an in-depth look at the BART whistleblowing incident from four perspectives: the engineers', management's, the directors', and the professional society's.[10] The most recent book, *Truth ... And Consequences: Seven Who Would Not Be Silenced*, is less ambitious and presents only the whistleblowers' perspectives[11] Based on hundreds of interviews, Greg Mitchell describes the fate of seven whistleblowers. Similarly, in *Serpico*, Peter Maas chronicles what happened to Frank Serpico, the detective who blew the whistle on the New York City Police Department.[12]

Scholarly Materials

Books and articles under the rubric of "scholarly materials" address principles of business, law, or ethics. Several representative examples will serve to illustrate each area.

In *Exit, Voice, and Loyalty*, Albert Hirshman argues that organizations frequently only provide two viable options for those who disagree with official policy: exit (leaving the organization) or loyalty (remaining with the organization quietly).[13] He suggests that organizations would be substantially improved by providing a "voice option," so that people could express their concerns in a constructive manner.

In *Bureaucratic Opposition: Challenging Abuses at the Workplace*, Deena Weinstein views organizations as political systems instead of as rational, neutral entities.[14] She maintains that most institutions lack the necessary procedures for handling dissent and have not recognized its legitimacy. Bureaucratic opposition is, therefore, interpreted as pathological behavior instead of as morally legitimate activity. David Ewing's *Freedom Inside the Organization* traces the history of civil liberties in this country and describes the forces that have kept them out of the workplace.[15] He suggests ways in which a new balance between employee rights and managerial prerogatives can be achieved. S. Pratash Sethi uses case studies in his book *Up Against the Corporate Wall* to illustrate the variety of problems that are increasingly becoming a concern to both business and society.[16] He attempts to develop the reader's sensitivity to the issues, the complexity of the motives, and a familiarity with the success and failure of business strategies and tactics.

Numerous articles in law reviews and legal journals offer theoretical analyses on the current state of the law regarding employee rights and protections. Phillip Blumberg examines statutes in both the United States and England concerning an employee's right to give opinions and information freely.[17] In "Protecting the Private Sector At-Will Employee Who 'Blows the Whistle,'" John Conway discusses the developing right of private sector employees to bring suit against the employer for retaliatory discharge.[18] Lawrence Blades focuses on the abusive exercise of employer power to discharge dissenting employees and examines the legal underpinnings of the employment-at-will doctrine.[19] Related to public employment, Mitchel Lindauer explores the disclosure rights of federal and state government employees by identifying each of the various substantive constitutional and statutory grounds.[20]

NOTES

1. Government Accountability Project, *A Whistleblower's Guide to the Federal Bureaucracy.* Washington, DC: Institute for Policy Studies, 1977.
2. Peter B. Broida, "How to Whistle," *The Government Standard* 37 (August 1979): 14.
3. Tekla Perry, "Knowing How to Blow the Whistle," *IEEE Spectrum*, 18 (September 1981): 56–61.
4. Peter Raven-Hansen, "Dos and Don'ts for Whistleblowers: Planning for Trouble," *Technology Review* 82 (May 1980): 34–44.
5. Rhonda Brown and Paul Matteucci, "The High Cost of Whistle-Blowing," *Inquiry*, September 1981, pp. 14–19.
6. Kermit Vandivier, "The Aircraft Brake Scandal," *Harper's Magazine*, April 1972, pp. 45–52.
7. Ernest A. Fitzgerald, *The High Priests of Waste*, New York: W.W. Norton, 1972.
8. Ralph Nader, Peter J. Petkas, and Kate Blackwell, eds., *Whistle-Blowing: The Report of the Conference on Professional Responsibility*, New York: Grossman Publishers, 1972.
9. Alan F. Westin, ed., *Whistle-blowing: Loyalty and Dissent in the Corporation*, New York: McGraw-Hill, 1980.
10. Robert M. Anderson, Robert Perrucci, Dan E. Schendel, and Leon E. Trachtman; eds., *Divided Loyalties: Whistle-Blowing at BART*, West Lafayette, Ind: Purdue University, 1980.
11. Greg Mitchell, *Truth . . . And Consequences: Seven Who Would Not Be Silenced*, New York: Dembner Books, 1981.
12. Peter Maas, *Serpico*, New York: Basic Books, 1973.
13. Albert L. Hirshman, *Exit, Voice, and Loyalty*, Cambridge: Harvard University Press, 1970.
14. Deena Weinstein, *Bureaucratic Opposition: Challenging Abuses at the Work Place*, New York: Pergamon Press, 1979.
15. David W. Ewing, *Freedom Inside the Organization*, New York: E.P. Dutton, 1977.
16. S. Prakash Sethi, *Up Against the Corporate Wall*, 4th ed., Englewood Cliffs, NJ: Prentice-Hall, 1981.
17. Phillip I. Blumberg, "Corporate Responsibility and the Employer's Duty of Loyalty and Obedience: A Preliminary Inquiry," *Oklahoma Law Review* 24 (August 1971): 279–318.
18. John Conway, "Protecting the Private Sector At-Will Employee Who 'Blows the Whistle': A Cause of Action Based Upon Determinants of Public Policy," *Wisconsin Law Review* 77 (1977): 777–812.
19. Lawrence Blades, "Employment At Will vs. Individual Freedom: On Limiting the Abusive Exercise of Employer Power," *Columbia Law Review* 67 (December 1967): 1404–1435.
20. Mitchel J. Lindauer, "Government Employee Disclosures of Agency Wrongdoing: Protecting the Right to Blow the Whistle," *University of Chicago Law Review* 42 (Spring 1975): 530–561.

ABOUT THE AUTHORS

FREDERICK A. ELLISTON, Associate Professor of Philosophy at the University of Hawaii, served as Principal Investigator for the project on whistleblowing that produced this volume. He holds a Ph.D. in philosophy from the University of Toronto and has taught at Trinity College, York University and the State University of New York at Albany. In addition to books on Husserl, Heidegger and Sartre he has published collections on crime, feminism and human sexuality. His most recent work deals with criminal justice ethics.

JOHN KEENAN, Dean of Business and Public Service Administration at Beaufort Technical College, was Research Associate on this project. Dr. Keenan taught previously at St. Rose College and Empire State College in New York. He has written on various topics in business, industry and professional life.

PAULA LOCKHART, Assistant to the Executive Director of Adult Learning at the State Department of Education in New York, served as Research Assistant on the whistleblowing project. She holds a Master's degree from the School of Criminal Justice at the State University of New York at Albany. She coauthored *Professional Dissent: An Annotated Bibliography and Resource Guide* with Drs. Elliston and Bowman.

JANE VAN SCHAICK also served as Research Assistant. She graduated from St. Rose College and is completing a MBA at the Illinois Institute of Technology. She is the Executive Director of the Chicago Research Institute and an Associate at the Institute for Business Ethics at DePaul University. She has conducted research on the quality of work life (QWL) and economic development and published *Legal Ethics: An Annotated Bibliography and Resource Guide* with Dr. Elliston.